Autobiography of
Glade Marvin Lyon

John Taylor Lyon and Gloy Miner Lyon on their honeymoon in 1922

Autobiography of Glade Marvin Lyon

Glade Marvin Lyon

WAKING LION PRESS

ISBN 978-1-4341-0389-5

Published by Waking Lion Press, an imprint of The Editorium

Waking Lion Press™, the Waking Lion Press logo, and The Editorium™ are trademarks of The Editorium, LLC

The Editorium, LLC
West Jordan, UT 84081-6132
wakinglionpress.com
wakinglion@editorium.com

Contents

Autobiography of Glade Marvin Lyon   1
Sugar City 13
Ashton 15
College 19
War 22
Marriage 35
Business and Community 40
The Point 53
Family Vacations 57
Businesses 59
Travel 65
Property 66
Mexico 67

Bowling	68
Church	69
Fun	71
Sickness	73
Hunting	73
More Business Ventures	74
Travel	75
Pets	75
Hunting and Camping	77
Teton Dam Disaster	85
Foreign Friends	87
Real Estate	87
Family Reunion	88
Computers	92
Further Developments	97

Military History   101

Glade Lyon and the National Guard 112

Mail from Glade to His Parents   115

Thursday 8:00 pm 115

Saturday afternoon 115

Tuesday nite 117

Sunday morning	118
Telegram	119
Saturday morning	120
Mar. 6, 1943	121
Mar. 18, 1943	122
Thursday nite	122
April 17, 1943	124
May 12, 1943	124
Aug. 9, 1943	125
August 16, 1943	127
North Camp Hood, Texas	129
Aug. 30 1943	130
Sunday night	130
Pvt. Glade M. Lyon	131
Pvt. Glade M. Lyon	133
Western Union	134
Saturday night	134
Date illegible 1943	134
Sept. 28, 1943	135
Tuesday morning	136
Wednesday morning	136
Pfc. Glade Lyon	138
Saturday afternoon	139
Saturday afternoon	141

Saturday evening	142
Sunday afternoon	143
Wednesday noon	144
Sunday afternoon	144
Feb. 21, 1944	145
Sunday afternoon	146
Saturday afternoon	148
Monday night	149
March 20, 1944	150
Tuesday afternoon	152
6–24–44	153
Monday noon	153
August 8, 1944	154
Telegram	155
Monday nite	155
Monday Evening	156
August 30, 1944	157
Sept. 7, 1944	158
Saturday morning	160
Sept. 12, 1944	161
Tuesday nite	162
Wednesday	163
Friday, Oct. 9, 1944 [mailed with above]	164
Wed. morning	165

Monday nite	166
Monday nite	168
Nov. 2, 1944	169
Nov. 16, 1944	170
Tuesday nite	171
Pfc. Glade M. Lyon	173
Dec. 17, 1944	174
Jan. 4, 1945	175
Jan. 8, 1945	175
Jan. 1, 1945	176
Jan. 2, 1945	177
Jan. 3, 1945	177
Feb. 9, 1945	178
Undated	179
April 5, 1945	180
April 29, 1945	180
May 5, 1945	181
May 6, 1945	182
May 8, 1945	182
May 22, 1945	183
June 1, 1945	183
June 11, 1945	184
July 10, 1945	184
18 July 1945	185

Written Aug. 2, 1945	185
Written Aug. 2, 1945	186
Aug. 30, 1945	186
Sept. 5, 1945	186
Sept. 13, 1945	188
September 29, 1945	189
Oct. 7, 1945	190
Oct. 10, 1945	190
Oct. 15, 1945	191
October 18, 1945	192
November 4, 1945	193
Nov. 16, 1945	195
Thanksgiving (Nov. 25, 1945)	196
Nov. 29, 1945	197
Dec. 8, 1945	199
Dec. 21, 1945	200
Feb 12, 1946	201

Grandpa Glade's Rules   203

Autobiography of Glade Marvin Lyon

I wish that I knew more about the lives of my parents and grandparents, so I'm going to attempt to write something about my life and times. Maybe my grandkids or greatgrandkids will enjoy reading it. Maybe not.

I was born on September 2, 1923 in our living quarters on the second floor of the Union Pacific Railroad depot in Tetonia, Idaho, to John Taylor Lyon (everybody called him Jack, except his relatives from Kansas who called him Taylor), and Gloy Opal Miner Lyon.

It was a Sunday and Mom and Dad had been on a picnic. When they realized it was time for me to come, they hurried back to town and looked for the doctor but couldn't find him and so a midwife, Lillian Mayette Hillman, assisted my mother in my birth. In many ways we had a better home than most of the people in the community, even though we lived on the second story of the Union Pacific depot, because the depot had burned down not long before and in re-building, most of the latest stuff, such as electricity, was incorporated. But we still cooked over a wood stove, and heated with a wood burning stove in the living room,

Railroad depot, Tetonia Idaho

and it was my job to bring the wood up from the main floor and to make sure I had chopped enough kindling to start the fire.

Saturday night was bath night (whether you needed it or not) in a round metal tub in the middle of the kitchen floor with water heated on top of the wood cooking stove. Kids got to use the bath water that parents had just finished with. I remember sleeping with my sister Carma in the hide-a-bed and on Sunday mornings we'd follow along while the man on the radio read the comics from the newspaper to us. I always hurried home from school to listen to "Little Orphan Annie" and "Jack Armstrong, the All American Boy" and "Og, Son of Fire" on the radio. "Little Orphan Annie" would always end with an encrypted message that you could decipher only with the Official Decoder Ring that you could get by sending in the seal from a bottle of Ovaltine. Wish I still had my ring.

Little Orphan Annie decoder ring from 1935

I remember having parties with my peers in the depot waiting-room and playing silly games like "spin the bottle" and "post office." When I was about ten, Dad got permission from the railroad and walled off part of the main-floor waiting room so I could have my own bedroom. That was wonderful.

Picnicing (we called it camping) is how we spent most of the summer Sundays during my childhood. Dad was the most avid of fishermen so we went camping every chance we got. I remember

Lyon family home in Willow Springs, Missouri. Left to right: Grandpa and Grandma Lyon (Algernon and Martha, parents of John Taylor Lyon), Gloy, young Glade, John Taylor

Glade with fish

once when Dad and Uncle Merlon got caught fishing on North Leigh (in Wyoming) without a license and had to pay a fine and then later go to Jackson Wyo. to buy their fishing gear back at public auction. I fished sometimes as I grew up but I preferred shooting the .22 rifle, so I shot at a lot of paper plates with a bulls-eye made with a piece of charcoal from our fire.

These trips usually included my maternal grandparents, Grandpa and Grandma Miner, and perhaps some of my mother's siblings, Verda (who died at age sixteen when I was six years old), and Merlon and Boyd and Fay and their spouses Edith and Lillian and Russell, and their kids.

I attended all eight grades of elementary school in Tetonia. We had the first three grades in one room, the fourth, fifth, and sixth in the middle room and the seventh and eighth in the third (big) room. In the first three grades, the desks faced east and I still have trouble realizing that the top of the map is not east. After school I usually stopped to visit at Grandpa's general merchandise store on the way home and see if I could get a free piece of candy. A big (1 1/2" x 2" x 1/2") solid piece of Nestle's chocolate was two cents and so was a "Guess What" which was two pieces of taffy and a small toy all wrapped together. Sometimes he'd give me a piece, but sometimes he'd refuse and I'd have to go ask grandma for an egg out of the chicken coop so I could trade it to Grandpa for a piece of candy. I always walked the quarter of a mile to school. Through three feet of snow and it was up-hill both coming and going. In the winter I could sometimes catch a ride back home to the depot on one of the runners (bobs) on the horse-team-pulled bob-sleigh that was taking the mail to the afternoon train.

Grandpa's store sold almost everything anyone needed. The shelves on the south side were full of canned goods and there was a counter that had bins full of beans and rice and macaroni, etc. and a display with a big round piece of cheese and a huge knife to cut off a piece. There was a wire rack full of boxes of cookies, each with its own glass lid, and a glass case that was full of candy. The north side of the store had fabrics and sewing notions and small clothing items. At the rear were the shoes and overalls and other major clothing items. In the middle was a huge pot-bellied stove with captain's chairs all around for the visitors. The telephone hung on the wall and you had to crank the ringer to get the operator and then tell her the number you were calling.

Miner family picnic. Left to right: Verda, Andrew Clinton, Glade, Lillian, Carma, Gloy, Mette Ann, John Taylor. The photographer was probably Boyd Miner, Lillian's husband

The back room had a barrel of kerosene (usually called coal-oil). When a customer brought in a gallon can for kerosene for their lamps, it would be filled from that barrel and then a potato would be forced on the spout for a cork. The dirt floor basement of the store was filled with cases of groceries. Out in front was a gas pump with a ten gallon glass container on top. A handle on the side of the tank had to be pushed from side to side to pump the gasoline up from the buried tank to fill that glass container with the amount of gas the customer wanted and it was then delivered to his tank by gravity. The Post Office was a separate (attached) building accessible from the front of the building as well as from the center of the north side of the store. Once when Grandpa went somewhere for a couple of weeks, I, at age thirteen, ran the Post Office. I'm pretty sure now that I had someone watching me very closely, but at that time I believed that I was running it single-handedly.

I spent a lot of time playing in and around the depot. I was a pretty good marble player and we used the hard-packed sand around the depot for marble rings or a marble game with holes dug in the sand to shoot the marbles into. There were always piles of sand nearby to make roads for our toy cars and to do sandpile things with. The inside of the far end of the loading dock was a perfect place for a hideout and I spent lots of time there. Guess I was kind of a loner although I think I had plenty of friends to play with. We spent lots of time making "rubber-guns" out of a pistol-shaped piece of wood with a clothes-pin on the back of the handle and rubber rings made out of old automobile inner-tubes (they were made of rubber then and were stretchy) to shoot. Cowboys and Indians or cops and robbers. The hills just northeast of town had lots of big rocks and were great for exploring. I remember spending a lot of time at my grandparent's home. I took piano lessons once (it was futile) and I always practiced there because we didn't have a piano. Between their house and the store was a big vacant lot where sometimes at night we kids would build

Grandpa and Grandma Miner (Andrew Clinton and Mette Ann, parents of Gloy Miner Lyon) in front of their store in Tetonia, Idaho; note gas pump on left and post office on right. Gloy's handwriting at the bottom

Interior of the Miner store, June 10, 1936. A.C. Miner with clerk Valoie Campbell

a bonfire and play games like kick-the-can and run-sheep-run around it, and occasionally toss in a few twenty-two rifle shells for excitement. And we'd make boats out of walnut shells or shingles with rubber-band-powered paddle wheels and float them in the ditch. I remember spending a lot of time playing in ant-hills, like putting candy on the end of a stick or on a string between two sticks and watching the ants get the candy. I did quite a bit of fly-fishing in Spring Creek just south of town beginning when I was about 8. I also spent a lot of time in the sagebrush field west of the depot shooting with Dad's .22 calibre model 37 Winchester, which he gave to me when I was about 12 and which I later gave to Jack, or trapping ground squirrels or "chislers" as we called them. The county would sometimes pay a bounty of a penny a tail for them and since .22 shells cost 25 cents for a box of 50, if you never missed, you could make pretty good money (and I never missed—well, hardly ever). I often had a cage with a chisler in it for a pet. I guess I was about six when they started the first movie theater in Driggs and I remember going to the silent movies there. There would always be an episode of a serial like "The Perils of Pauline" with a cliff-hanger-ending every time so you'd be sure to come to the next show to find out how she was saved. Then came sound and that was great. I was about ten when they opened the theater in Tetonia. I remember that at Sacrament meeting we all drank from a silver goblet passed along from one to another. No wonder we had a lot of sickness. I always had jobs selling weekly magazines like Colliers and Saturday Evening Post, and delivering them, and working in Grandpa's store. In the summer it was my job to bring Grandpa's cow in from the pasture. I was twelve before I got my first bike (for my birthday) and I used it to deliver magazines.

Carma and Glade

Sugar City

Just after I finished the eighth grade, Dad bid in the job of agent at Sugar City and we moved there. We still had to go outside to an outhouse to the toilet. The inside of the far end of the loading platform was still a good hide-away and I spent a lot of time there. I remember building wooden boxes that had lids that appeared to be nailed shut but had secret ways to open them. I got a job delivering the Salt Lake Tribune on Sundays to make a little spending money. I started high-school in Sugar City in 1937 and it was hard with no friends (nor acquaintances really) but I got along. I was really mad when I found out that I was required to take a religion course, and I guess I was pretty belligerent about that. I remember taking boy's home-ec and making cream of celery soup that was really good. My mother thought I should take a tap-dancing course that someone there was giving, so I did, but about all I learned was that I had two left feet. While we lived in Sugar City, my sister Carma, who was five years younger than I, got pneumonia. The elders came and gave her a blessing and promised her that she would be okay. When she died a few days later (at age nine), I was pretty bitter, and I guess I never got over it. It must have been really hard for my parents, especially my dad, for she was the apple of his eye. My sister Connie was born in December 1934, and I'm sure Carma's death enhanced my parents' love for Connie. She was eleven years younger than I, so we didn't play together much. My half-brother JT, (dad's son by his first marriage) eleven years older than I, came to visit us one summer in Tetonia, but I was seven and he was eighteen so we didn't have a lot in common. JT came for Dad's funeral in 1947 and we got acquainted and I now feel like we are brothers and that his daughter Shari is my niece.

JT Lyon

Glade, Connie, and Carma at the Sugar City depot. Gloy's handwriting at the bottom

Ashton

Dad didn't like the job in Sugar City, so when the agent's job in Ashton opened up a year later, he bid it in. I started my sophomore year in Ashton in 1938, and again, it was hard not knowing anyone. Guess I was kind of a radical (I once met with the school board to try to get them to change our class scheduling) but I got along. Ashton High had never had a Yearbook so I instituted and became the editor-in-chief of the first one, the 1941 Husky Howl. I was elected president of the Senior class, so ever since I've been the one they look to for reunions, etc.

I've always told my kids that if you need a job and can't find one you may be able to create one. Right after we moved to Ashton, I went into Stone's grocery store to ask for a job. He told me they didn't need any help. But I noticed that they had just received their weekly shipment of groceries and the boxes were all stacked in the aisles. I said I'd unpack them and mark them and put the

Home of John Taylor and Gloy Lyon in Ashton

groceries on the shelves, but he said they could handle it. When I told him I'd do it for nothing, he let me do it. I did a good job, so when I went back the next week he hired me. Later, I found out that another grocery store was paying 35 cents a dozen for eggs and I knew I could buy them for 25 cents in Tetonia and it cost 75 cents to ship a thirty dozen case on the train. That meant $3.00 gross profit less shipping of 75 cents totaled $2.25 net profit (the best job I could find paid $1.00 per day!) so I made more than two days wages with hardly any effort. The problem was, they'd only buy a case a week at most. I worked for awhile at Nels Knudsen's grocery store (later to become Lyon's store) where

Glade in his teens

Ashton High School

one of my jobs was to "candle" eggs. The farmers would bring in eggs and trade them for groceries and I would take them into a little back room and hold them in front of a light globe to inspect them to see if they were starting to turn into chickens yet. If they were, we'd throw them out but if not, they'd be put out for sale. I worked at the City Drug as a soda-jerk for a long time. In the back room there was a hole cut through the wall into Lyd's Cafe so I could order a hot roll for my breakfast or they could order a milk-shake if one of their customers wanted one. For a while I opened at 7:00 A.M. I remember sometimes getting there for work without having gone to bed. Those Warm River dances!!

College   19

The Rendezvous dance hall at Warm River

College

I graduated from Ashton High School in 1941 and that fall I went to the University of Idaho in Moscow to school. I'd always liked math and chemistry so I majored in Chemical Engineering. It was interesting and I got along okay, with a grade point average between 3 and 3.5 (I still have my class schedule that shows I once carried 24 credit hours). I spent a lot of time shooting pool. At home I had had a small pool table in my bedroom and my Dad had taught me how to play. When I played "pea pool" for dimes and quarters on a full size table it was *so* easy. I made a lot of spending money that way. Had to be careful not to win too much or they didn't want to play anymore. I met a Moscow high-school girl named Mildred "Benny" Eide and we had a lot of fun together—jitter-bugging mostly. We got engaged, but that was just dumb kid stuff because I was going away to war.

The summer after I graduated from high school I worked for Uncle Russ Rammell in his grocery store in Tetonia and lived with Grandpa and Grandma Miner. On Saturday nights we never planned to close until about ten at night but didn't usually make it that early. One of my jobs was to make sure there was a case of six ounce bottles of cold Squirt to go with the half-gallon of gin Dan Linderman usually brought in about closing time. We joked that the way to drink Squirt was to take a drink and then fill the

Science Hall at the University of Idaho, postcard, 1941

bottle with gin and then another drink and again fill the bottle with gin. By the time you were drinking almost straight gin it didn't matter anymore. I remember one time we got a phone call at about eleven at night, and I can still hear Uncle Russ saying "yeah we got 'em, yeah they'll be ready when you get here," and then he turned to me and said "there's two dozen chickens in a cage in the back room, go kill 'em." I had them plucked and drawn and ready to cook by the time the guy from the restaurant in Jackson got there. I also remember that the little cafe across the street served a great hamburger and a milk shake for 25 cents.

One summer night between college terms I took a gal from Chester to the dance at Warm River. We had a good time and started back to town a few minutes before the dance ended so I could get her home before it was really late. It was raining hard. Just after going through Marysville, I saw headlights coming toward me. They didn't blind me but they did distract me for a moment (it was the first car we'd seen) and when I looked back at the road there was a man in dark clothing right in front of me.

Typical "Galloping Goose," an automobile fitted with railroad wheels and used to pull passenger or other cars that were too small to need a full-fledged locomotive

I tried to turn left to miss him (don't know why I didn't hit the oncoming car or what ever happened to it) but I did hit him with the right front fender. I stopped but I couldn't find him in the dark. I stopped a couple of cars coming from the dance and sent for the police. They finally came. He had been seen a little earlier staggering and falling down a couple of times crossing the street in Ashton as he left the bar. They never even held an inquest, but I never ever pass there but what I think about it.

The summer between my first and second years of college, I worked for the Union Pacific railroad. It was my job to clean the "Galloping Goose" that carried passengers to Victor and back, and anything else the boss could think up. One day I went to work and they showed me a train-car-load of lump coal and gave me a

Steam locomotive at the Ashton train depot

shovel and told me to throw the coal through that hole up there on the roof of the coal bin. It took me three days and you can't imagine how glad I was to be finished. The next morning when I got to work there was another car-load ready to be emptied the same way. And I got to do it. But the day the boss told me to go fire up the big steam engine and take it down to the wye and turn it around and bring it back made up for everything else.

War

On December 7, 1941, the Japs bombed Pearl Harbor without warning and everyone was ready to go to war. But I finished that school year and started my sophomore year before I enlisted. Jim Barber and I went down to the Recruiting Office and joined the Army (I tried to join the Air Force but my eyes weren't good enough) on November 2, 1942 (right after I turned 19), but then they said that it might be a long war and they might need engineers worse than they needed riflemen so they'd let us know

Glade going off to war. Gloy, Glade, Connie, and John Taylor

when they wanted us. We were so mad! The next June they called us to active duty. We went by train from Moscow to Salt Lake City (I was in Ashton, and had to go back to Moscow because that's where I had enlisted) and were inducted at Fort Douglas. A couple of weeks there and then to some tar-paper shacks at North Camp Hood near Waco, Texas for three months of infantry basic training.

I'd had two years of ROTC (Reserve Officer's Training Corp.) at U of I so they made me a platoon sergeant (but neglected to give me the stripes that should have gone with the job) almost immediately. Jim Barber and I were good friends from college but he was always a little overbearing until we took the AGCT (IQ) test. When they posted the scores and I had 145 and he had 144, his attitude changed instantly. The training was tough, with obstacle courses, infiltration courses, hand-to-hand combat, forced marches, rifle range, etc., etc., all in central Texas weather the last half of June, July, August and the first half of September (they told us once that it had been 135 degrees that day), but most of us made it[1] and entrained for Lehigh University in Bethlehem, Pennsylvania (there was four inches of snow on the ground when we arrived and we had only our summer uniforms and we thought we were going to freeze to death) where we took a third-year course in Electrical Engineering. One day they took us to the swimming pool and said all swimmers over there and the rest of you over there. I couldn't swim but was scared to learn so I went over with the swimmers. Then they said "prove it" so I went back with the others. I got so I could swim as long as I could hold my breath (once across the pool) but that was about all. I've always wished I could really swim and so I've made sure my kids learned how and bugged my kids to make sure their kids learned how.

In Bethlehem we were only about an hour from New York City, so I hitch-hiked there quite often. It was great for a kid from the sticks. New Year's Eve 1943/1944 on Times Square was a never-to-be-forgotten experience. The people were packed together so tightly you couldn't fall down if you'd wanted to. In Bethlehem, I met Margie Bedicks and we had a lot of fun together, and got engaged. That was dumb but it just seemed the thing to do when you were going away to war. Then on to Fort Monmouth, New Jersey to the Signal Corps Training School where Barber (he usually called me MacLyon) and I got split up because our names started with different letters. We did a lot of training on telephones and "carrier bays" (a casket sized box full of electronic stuff that weighed 700 pounds but had six handles so the army called it portable equipment). We had four voice (telephone) channels, and could substitute four teletype for any one. We also had facsimile capability (now called FAX). In

---

1. Glade later recalled that they were warned not to drink too much water after coming in from the heat. One of the men ignored the warning, drank lots of water, and ate some ice cream. A few hours later, he was dead.

Times Square, New Year's Eve, 1943

the fall of 1944 we lived in tents in New Jersey in the rain on field maneuvers and on the first of December of 1944 we took a Liberty Ship from New York to Liverpool, England. The North Atlantic in December was really rough. We bounced around a lot in that little ship and worried a lot about whether we would be torpedoed by Nazi submarines, but we arrived safely. Most of the guys got sea-sick but I never did. We lived in quarters at Aintree Race Track, near Liverpool. I was one of the very few that got a package from home for Christmas; a box of crumbs that had been sugar cookies from Grandma Miner (they were delicious). We spent most of our time guarding the docks while the supply ships were being unloaded. We were on twelve hour shifts and one time our replacements didn't show up, so we worked our shift and then their shift and then ours again without our regular rations (we broke open a crate of oranges to have something to eat). The sailors on a Destroyer Escort tied up there saw our problem and invited us on board for breakfast. We had been having Spam and powdered eggs and hard biscuits and lousy coffee full of chicory every morning, so when they gave us a menu and asked how we wanted our eggs, we were ready to join the Navy.

While we were in Liverpool the D'Oyly Carte Opera Company was presenting all the Gilbert and Sullivan Operettas and my friend Sergeant James from Florida invited me to go to them with him. It was absolutely fascinating! Everyone wore their finest, tuxes and evening gowns (we were in uniform) and I was entranced and enamored with the music and the lyrics. We were in Liverpool for a couple of months and saw most of the plays. I remember one night walking to the theater in dense fog when suddenly the air-raid siren sounded and all the lights of the city were turned out immediately. I've never seen it so dark. I couldn't see my hand in front of my face, so we sort of felt our way to the theater. I met a girl named Sybil Hughes in Liverpool and had some great dates with her. I got a three day pass to London and had a good time there even though one night I left my billfold with all my money and identification in it under my pillow at the YMCA (never did get it back). I saw an unexploded German V-2 rocket half buried in the street and heard others going off in the distance at irregular intervals. I bought a "Bowie" type knife in case I had to do any hand-to-hand fighting and a pair of side-cutter pliers to cut barbed wire with. Luckily, I never had to use either one.

Then we entrained for South Hampton where we boarded a troop ship (think of me climbing a rope net up the side of the ship with a pack on my back and carrying a rifle and a duffel bag) and went across the channel, and then on some motor launches up the Seine River to an army camp called Twenty Grand. We slept there one night in our sleeping bags that were one layer of army blanket in a thin canvas shell (I put a bucket of water by my bed so I'd be ready to shave in the morning but it had an inch of ice on it when I woke up). The next morning we marched for a couple

Sergeant Lyon

of hours to a small town where we got on a train in box-cars marked "Quarante Hommes ou Huit Cheveaux" (Forty Men or Eight Horses). We spent two days and one night on the train but there wasn't room for everyone to lie down at the same time so three of us sat most of the night with our feet hanging out the open door, singing "By the Light of the Silvery Moon." At noon on the second day of that train trip we had just received the C-rations for our lunch when we stopped at the station in a small town. When I saw a man come around the corner of the station and sit down on the ground to eat his meal I jumped off the train and offered to trade him. I've always said that that loaf of home-made french bread (complete with chaff) and the bottle of red wine he had were one of the best meals of my life. When we got to Verdun we detrained and got de-loused (sprayed with DDT) (even though we didn't think we needed it) and then ten of us went in two trucks to Saarbrucken, Germany for our first assignment. Five of us set up a telephone communications post there, in what had been German Army headquarters (the roof was eight feet of solid concrete), with the other five men on a nearby hill with a radio to transmit our telephone messages (usually from SHAEF—Supreme Headquarters Allied Expeditionary Forces) to the repeaters and then on to the final destination (usually to Division headquarters). We had the most sophisticated electronic equipment of the time (telephones, teletypes, and facsimile (FAX)) and our Battalion (the 3186th Signal Service Bn.) supplied communications for all of the Allied Armies in Europe. Since generators were required to operate our equipment, we always had electricity for lights and cooking or whatever. I learned later that we were the first unit of our battalion to go into Germany.

We had been in Saarbrucken for about three days, when, as we drove down the street, we saw someone duck into a partially bombed-out building. We followed him because we didn't want to get shot in the back. We never found him but we did find a huge wine cellar. There were about fifteen wooden casks, each about eight feet high and twelve feet in length, each with, it seemed, a different kind of wine. We lived three blocks from the wine cellar and five miles from the nearest watering point (it was no contest). It's amazing how much better you eat when you take two five gallon cans of wine with you to trade on your weekly trip to the ration dump. We "liberated" cookware, dishes, glassware, tableware, or whatever we needed from nearby houses. Months later, after the war was over, we happened to go through Saarbrucken, so we stopped to get some more wine. There was a guard at the door who said we couldn't go in, and besides he said, "tank trucks had come and taken all the wine." When I said "I bet they missed one cask that I know of," he let us in. Sure enough, back in a corner there was one full wine cask. We couldn't find a bung-starter so I used my rifle barrel to knock the bung in and got soaked with wine in the process, but we got our five gallon cans filled. We left behind one really happy guard.

    About three weeks after we got to Saarbrucken, an infantry company moved into town. They were the first soldiers we had seen since we got there. When we asked them what they were doing there, they said they had been sent to "hold the town." Made us wonder what we had been doing. A few days after that, we were walking down the street toward the old German headquarters which we had taken over, when a German machine gun started firing at a truck convoy crossing a bridge about four blocks away. At first we thought we'd grab our rifles and go help but then we decided that was the job of the infantry company. So we let them do it. One day three of us went up on the hill to our radio terminal to visit and to see if we could find a deer. While we were out hunting we saw three men approaching and we could see that one had a rifle, which was strictly forbidden. We stepped back off the road and when they got to us we stopped them. They had the rifle, a pair of binoculars, and a pistol. I took the pistol, a seven shot revolver (what a neat gun for a Western movie!), which appeared to be Russian, but I couldn't find ammunition

Allied invasion of Saarbrucken, 1941

for it so after the war ended I traded it for a 6.35 mm Mauser pistol. When we got to the Philippines I had a shoulder holster made for it and carried it after I saw a bar fight that demonstrated how efficient the Filipinos were with their butterfly-knives. I once read that that seven shot revolver was probably Czechoslovakian and worth a lot of money.

We moved around quite a bit in Germany. One of the towns we were in was Wetzlar, home of the Leica camera factory. I bribed a guy to go into the factory and find a camera or enough parts to build one but he couldn't, but finally said he had a friend who had one. I gave the friend one dozen candy bars and five cartons of cigarets for an old Leica camera which I later sold (after the iris diaphragm had rusted going across the Pacific) in Japan for

$165.[2] When we left Wetzlar we were short of space so I had to leave behind a duffel bag filled with candy and cigarets. I've often wondered about that really lucky fellow who found that bag.

Another time we moved and ten of us set up both telephone and radio equipment on top of a hill, using a little castle-type building for our equipment and living in a tent big enough to handle about 24 men. For our defense we had a .50 calibre machine gun on an anti-aircraft mount. We had been there a few days when suddenly a small German bi-plane with a bomb under each wing started circling us. Some of the guys wanted to try to shoot it down but I was the ranking non-com and I said "no, unless he drops his bombs." We had trained with that particular weapon, but I had never seen anyone hit anything with it. I had a few anxious moments before he decided we weren't a good enough target.

Once they asked me and another guy to deliver the mail to some of the rest of our battalion. We had a "weapons carrier" (an over-sized jeep) and took off. We had a map, but it wasn't too long before we were afraid we were lost (all the signs were in German), but we kept on going and suddenly we came into a small town and found ourselves completely surrounded by German soldiers. We were really glad when we realized that none of them had weapons. They were all prisoners of war.

Three of us were once assigned to an area near the Belgian border where the British had a switchboard which we tied into, and so I was attached to the British Second Army for a while. We arranged it so we were each on duty 24 hours and off 48 so I was able to hitch-hike to Brussels once. I was also able to contact Jim Barber who was running a switchboard in Marseilles, France, but I had to tell the switchboard operators in Paris it was official army business before they'd patch me through. I hadn't heard from him directly since we were separated in New Jersey. We were in Essen, Germany when the war ended in May 1945,

---

2. Glade later recalled that he went around Germany asking store owners, "Haben-sie ein Fotoapparat? Ein Leica?"

and then went to Weisbaden to wait for orders. There the Red Cross took over the fanciest building in town and had coffee and doughnuts for fifteen cents, while the Salvation Army had a much smaller building down the street a few blocks where coffee and doughnuts were free. So, whenever I feel like making a donation, the Salvation Army gets it. After a couple of weeks we convoyed to Arles, France (where, in a small bar, I discovered Amaretto, a delicious almond flavored liqueur) where we set up a tent city in the desert and spent a month waiting for a ship. But while we were waiting, I was able to get into Marseilles and get drunk with Barber a couple of times.

Then they put us on an ocean liner (the Matsonia) converted to a troop ship and took us through the Panama Canal (stayed one night in Panama City, first time we'd seen sheets for months) and on to Manila, Philippine Islands, where we first set up camp in a mosquito infested swamp (I spent three days in a hospital with athlete's foot). It was there I bought "Murgatroyd" my little monkey. She was a lot of fun—especially when she'd sit on my shoulder and wet—but I sold her when we left. After a week or two we were sent to Linguayen Gulf, a beautiful beach, where for about a month we had to sleep, pitch horseshoes, swim, body-surf, or play bridge (tough duty but somebody had to do it). One evening, some of my buddies told me there was a crap game in the mess hall and suggested I go and break it up. I went, and in about an hour I had won all the money and broken up the game. It was so idyllic there that when they said they needed a truck driver, I volunteered. I drove the six-by-six truck around the island a little, but didn't know much about how to do it. Then we were sent to Japan on an LST (Landing Ship Tank) with the vehicles on the lower deck. We were in the edge of a typhoon along the way and I remember the sailors telling me that sometimes in such high seas these ships would break in half. I knew they were kidding so I didn't worry about it, but I found out later that it did happen on occasion. When we got to Japan I drove the truck out

Ocean liner Matsonia

onto the sandy beach in third gear and immediately got stuck. The other vehicles went around me and I slowly worked my way out only to find that they had all gone and left me and I didn't know whether to turn right or left when I got to the main road. I chose to the right, and we were soon in a tiny town where all the people came running out to look at us so I was pretty sure we had gone the wrong way. I turned around and drove for awhile and suddenly could see a convoy way ahead going perpendicular to our direction. When I got to them I pulled into the convoy only three trucks behind my original position. When we stopped I asked where they had been and the other drivers said they had been driving all the time. They had been as lost as I was.

Our barracks were at Koshien Stadium, a football stadium halfway between Kobe and Osaka. Japan was very interesting even though there was so much bomb damage. I went into Kobe quite often to shop but the stores had very little to sell. Most of our shopping was done on the streets in tin shacks where they were selling black market stuff. We could buy a case of Asahi Japanese beer at our little PX for $2 and sell it to a Jap at a hole in the fence for $20, being careful not to get caught. We bought cigarettes at the PX for five cents a pack and easily sold them for $2. Our battalion held a golf tournament and I was lucky enough to win the first prize of a samurai sword of the type that the Japanese officers were issued. One day as we were emptying our plates into garbage cans after lunch, I noticed a little old gray-haired man and woman dipping their little buckets into the garbage cans and hurrying to eat as they turned away. I followed them to their nearby home and then started taking food to them. I even spent one night in their home sleeping on a straw mat. When I told them I was going home, they gave me their family samurai sword in a plain wooden scabbard. I found out later that it was over three hundred and fifty years old. One night I went to a dance that was advertised for the GI's and met a girl named Sumiko Kobayakowa. She was sweet and I felt sorry for her. Her family had sold her to the people who owned the dance hall. We spent a lot of time together wandering around Kobe. She later told me that her name was really Kazue Asahi but she had taken the other name as sort of a stage name. About the first of February 1946 they told me I had enough "points" for discharge, so they put me on a troop ship. They told us that we could not take any more money home with us than our army pay had totaled while we had been in Japan and we couldn't send it home (they lied) so I took the $1000 I had made gambling and selling on the black market and bought diamonds and pearls and a bolt of silk and brought it all home. We landed in San Francisco without much fanfare except an army band. Then went by train to Fort Lewis, Washington where I was discharged on Feb. 14, 1946 and then home by train.

   I've always been sorry that I never learned to swim growing up in Teton Valley and I was always scared of the water, so when I enlisted, I joined the Army because I didn't want anything to do with the Navy. My old high school buddy Gene Hemming joined the Navy to see the world. They gave him a two week shake-down cruise around Catalina Island and then left him as a hospital corpsman in San Diego the rest of the war. I went across the north Atlantic in a Liberty Ship, then across the channel on a troop ship and up the Seine River in a motor launch and later through the Mediterranean and across the Atlantic and through the Panama Canal and across the Pacific to the Philippines on the Monterrey (a Matson liner converted to a troop ship) and then to Japan on an LST (Landing Ship Tank) and finally back across the Pacific on a troop ship to San Francisco. A total of ninety days at sea.

Marriage

While I was in Germany, my folks had bought the store which was called Ashton Mercantile. I had intended to go back to college and get my engineering degree, but school didn't start until September (no block plans in those days) so I went to work in the store (without pay because the store couldn't afford me). It was kind of funny, because the folks had $800 when they bought the store, and when I got home I had $800, which I lived on for the ten months until Katie and I got married, so I always felt like the store was half mine. But by that fall, Dad's asthma was worse so Mom took him to Arizona to try to find a place he could breathe easier. They didn't find such a place and Dad died in July of 1947. In the meantime, I went into the drugstore for a coke one day in the spring of 1946 and asked this cute soda-jerk if she still loved me (we'd never dated before) and she said yes, so we got married on the first of December (it was getting too cold to sit out in the car and neck). Best move I ever made! I don't think her parents were overjoyed, but I'm sure mine were. I smoked (worst move I ever made) and drank a little and didn't go to church much, if at all, so I don't blame them. I'm really surprised that she's been able to tolerate me all these years.

After Katie and I got married we lived with my folks for awhile

Katie Murdoch

Marriage

because we couldn't find any place to rent, but finally we were able to rent a tiny apartment in the upstairs of Gus Lenz's home on the corner of 5th and Idaho, and then later a better one on the third floor of the Ashton Hotel where we shared a bathroom with Mary and Ivan Crouch. Then Vernon Rich asked if we wanted to buy the basement house he had just built for $5000, so we did. We had previously bought the corner lot next to it (corner of 5th and Fremont) from Jack Young and planned to build on it but then decided to buy the basement house. When Stan Clark came and offered us $750 for our corner lot (we'd paid $450) we needed the money so bad that we took it (been sorry ever since) (remember, I was making $175 a month). We lived in it for about four or five years while we saved up enough to build on up. I hired a carpenter named Wayne Josephson to teach me how to build a house. Jack was born in June of that year (1951). The carpentry was so noisy that we had to move back to my folk's home so he could sleep. It was a hard summer. I'd get up early and be pounding nails before 7:00 A.M. Wayne would come at 8:00. At about 2:00, I'd go to the store for a couple of hours and try to do the work that had to be done and then back to building. Wayne would quit at 5:00 but I'd keep on working until about 9:00 and then home for supper and fall into bed. About two A.M. I'd get up to give the baby a bottle. But we finally finished and really enjoyed our new home.

Right after we moved into the basement house, we bought one of the first electric blankets (actually, it was a rayon comforter) and had it on our bed. One night it stormed really hard and our flat roof started leaking right into the middle of the bed. We were wondering if it was dangerous when suddenly the wind blew a tree limb across the power line outside our bedroom window and the resulting flash made us think we'd been electrocuted. As soon as we found out we weren't dead we thought it was funny.

After we'd been married about three years, we went to Colorado to visit Bob (my best man) and Yutonna Bean. One day, Bob said

Katie and Glade, newlyweds

he had to go into Denver on business and wanted me to go with him. I said "okay, but I need to shave and clean up first" and he said "no, we're going right now." We went to the tenth floor of a fancy office building where the secretary turned up her nose and asked if we were there about employment. Unshaven Bob in his dirty, worn levis said "well, sort of, I want your boss to build me a quarter of a million dollar elevator." The secretary's change of attitude was instant and hilarious. Moral: you can't judge a book by its cover.

We'd been married for more than four years before Jack was born and we were beginning to think that we'd never have any kids and so we were really tickled when he arrived and again when Suzanne came along about two years later and then four years later we got Robin and then four more and Kathy showed up. They were all super special and we love them dearly. One guy told me that if he'd known how much fun grandkids were he'd have skipped the kids altogether, but I've always loved the kids—and the grandkids almost as much. I regret that I didn't spend more time with the kids as they grew up, but it seemed I was always too busy.

Soon after I got home from the service, a National Guard unit was formed (Company C, 116th Combat Engineers) and I joined because we drilled for about two hours a week and got paid a day's Army pay. I was a platoon sergeant and it wasn't too bad. We went on maneuvers for two weeks every summer to Fort Lewis or some such place. Then in 1951 our unit was called up to go to Korea. I had just been made Company First Sergeant and I had my duffel bag packed and I was ready to go when I was called back for a second physical exam. The X-rays showed a spot on my lung, so I was discharged because they said I might have tuberculosis. Dr. Krueger made tests and said I didn't have TB. When I told that to Capt. Cordon, our commanding officer, he said all I had to do was sign here and I could go with them. But I had a new

Suzanne, Robin, and Jack with new baby Kathy

baby, and a store to run, so I told him I'd already been to the far east so they could go without me.

Business and Community

The years passed and I was always busy. I was elected president of the Chamber of Commerce about 1956 and the first thing I did was double the dues from $10 to $20 per year. Everyone grumbled, but I only lost one member. Then I set up an agenda that had a different event for every month of the year. They included Ashton's first 4th of July fireworks display (dropped because of the cost of insurance), and the first Easter Egg Hunt (they're still doing it), and the first kid's parade (still done but at a different time of year), etc. Once we had a beard growing contest and the judges said mine was the best but since I was so involved in the Chamber they thought I should be disqualified.

Glade and Katie during the Idaho Centennial

My dad was always active in the American Legion. I went to Lewiston to a State Convention with him when I was about 15, so it was natural for me to join the Legion as soon as I was discharged from the army. I've always been quite active in the organization. About 1958, Ray McBride, the Commander, called a meeting to announce that he was moving to Rexburg and someone would have to take the job as Commander. I was the only prospect that turned up so I reluctantly took the job. No one wanted to come to meetings so I called a bunch of my friends, including Hal Harrigfeld and Hugh Hammond and told them we were going to have a poker game at the Legion Hall. When they and the others got there, I made them hold a meeting first. The organization has been going pretty well ever since. But the meetings got in the way of our card games so for the past 30 years or so we have been having a card game every Tuesday evening. HughB and I usually get there first and play cribbage until someone else comes and then we play Solo (a three or four player game, which by the way, is the best card game I have ever played) until we have four or five players, when it degenerates into a game we sometimes call poker (we play every wild game known to man). But we sure have fun. I've been keeping track for the past four years and I've won about $200 each year. Now that's fun.

I've been Commander of the Ashton American Legion Post twice and Seventh District Commander twice and was Department (State) Vice Commander under my good friend Elton Ashton (who later died from cancer due to smoking) from Malad for one year. I was appointed to the National Internal Affairs Commission (a really sought after position) on the recommendation of Harry Harn from Dubois, and served on it for five years. I attended meetings at the National Headquarters in Indianapolis twice a year and had a great time while learning a lot about the American Legion. I was not reappointed for my third three year term on the Internal Affairs Commision because I stood up for a principle I thought was being abused at the National Convention in New

Glade (right) with Legion buddies. Third from the left is Hugh Hammond (HughB), Glade's good friend

Orleans. They say you can't fight City Hall, but I believe you must stand up for what you think is right. My dad told me to help the guy on the bottom of the heap because the guy on top can take care of himself. I considered running for Department Commander but Kathy was still at home and I didn't want to spend that much time away from her. Sometimes I'm sorry I didn't go on up the ladder. I've always said the job I want most is Past Department Commander. I'm now on the National Cemetery Committee, which is almost the same as nothing, but it did get me a call-in (which means they pay your transportation and your hotel bill) to the 1995 National Convention in Indianapolis and to the National meetings in October 1997 (but mostly to help with the hospitality room for Al Lance's bid for National Commander) and the National meetings in Washington, D.C. in March 1998 and to Indy in May 1998.

Suzanne, Kathy, and Robin having fun

Along in there somewhere, Katie and I decided that her mother needed some improvements to her house, so I hired someone to pour the foundation and then grabbed my saw and hammer and remodeled her bathroom and added a bedroom on the ground floor so she wouldn't have to climb the stairs to get to her bedroom. She was really grateful. Why do we wait so long to do something to help someone?

Katie and I went to the National Legion Convention in Portland, Oregon in 1970 and on my birthday we took John and Ruth Blackburn a hundred miles to Newport for clam chowder at Mo's (they thought I was crazy, but the clam chowder was great) and we feasted on wild blackberries along the way. We took Kathy with us to the 1980 National Convention in Boston and walked the Freedom Trail and then went on to the Dominican Republic for about a week. We went to the National Convention in New Orleans and played pinochle with Lynn and Ruth Kearsley every time we

Business and Community

Glade and Katie at American Legion National Convention

sat down. We went to the National Convention in Salt Lake City where I dreamed up and was in charge of the baked potato giveaway, and where I was able to plant the seeds with my friend National Commander James Dean that led to Lynn Kearsley's (he's a really great guy) appointment as National Chaplain a few years later. In 1982 I went to Chicago to the National Convention without Katie. That was the time that Jay Phillips and I decided to visit the Playboy Club. Vangie Burkhalter wanted to go with us and we told her okay but when we got in the cab, the big black cab driver said "yeah, I know where it is but I wouldn't take my wife there" and I said "that's okay, I'm not."

A few years ago I found out that there is a special headstone for Medal of Honor (MOH) recipients and that some of them in Idaho did not have that special stone. So I compiled a pamphlet of all the MOH recipients of Idaho and began writing letters to various American Legion Posts around the state to make sure that those

MOH recipients had that special stone. It's taken a half-dozen years, but finally, they all have that special recognition.

I've been the chairman of the Flag Education Committee for the Ashton American Legion Post for several years and also for the Department of Idaho. I'm currently attempting to write a booklet about flag etiquette and flag history for use in the schools.

The Ashton American Legion has been using the "Community Birthday Calendar" as a fund raiser for many years. When I got my computer, I inherited from Misseldines the job of putting all the names and birthdates together. I'd already been selling the ads to the merchants, so now I get to do about everything except deliver most of them, and several of the other members help me with that. It's a good source of revenue for the Legion; we make about $2500 on it yearly, but it takes a lot of my time.

When Robin was 15 she told us that she was going to marry Verl Miller as soon as she turned 16. When we said "no," she said "how come all my friends are getting pregnant so they can get married and when I want to do it right and get married in the temple you won't let me?" Tough question (veiled threat?). We finally said "yes" but told her that she had to accompany us on a trip back east first. She didn't want to but we prevailed, so Katie and I and Suzanne and Robin and Kathy drove to Sudbury, Massachusetts and visited Connie and Ralph. Visited the Sacred Grove (neat place) and the Carthage Jail (where the only other outfit in the parking lot turned out to be Katie's nephew Dallas Earl and his family), etc. along the way. We picked up Sallie and went on to Quebec (no, they don't all speak English) and then back to Sudbury. I ate a fried clam that was past his prime in Durgin's Park in Boston and heaved all over Bunker Hill. Ate lobster in Rockport, Maine and steamed (over a bon-fire) the clams we dug on the beach at Cape Cod. Had a crumby hotel room in New York City, climbed the Statue of Liberty, took a walk in Central Park, visited Times Square, and visited the New York Stock Exchange on Wall Street where Robin stood at an observation window and

Glade, Katie, and daughters on trip

got a standing ovation from the guys on the floor of the exchange (at age 15 she was exceptionally beautiful). Wonder how many times, if ever, before or since, that that has happened? Then to Gettysburg, PA to visit Wallace and Pauline, and to "Idaho Day" which turned out to be a day-long visit with Senator Frank Church and his wife Bethene at their cabin in the hills. When my girls watched him feed a stray blind dog that wandered by, they decided he was okay. We climbed the Washington Monument and checked out some of the exhibits at the Smithsonian (you can pass on the Modern Art Museum) and stood in awe at the Lincoln Memorial while we listened to a mocking bird. When we got home Robin and Verl got married and had two boys before they divorced. I believe the main reason for their divorce was that at age sixteen she was not yet ready for marriage.

So many of our customers in "Lyon's" were Mexicans that I

decided to try to learn to speak Spanish. Robin and I took a night class at Rick's College and Katie and I and Robin took a couple of classes from Bonnie and her husband, Tito Paredes in St. Anthony. Katie and I learned a little and Robin learned a lot. Then Rodolfo spent a lot of time at the Orange Mart teaching her. That led to her divorce from Verl and her marriage to Rodolfo. It was a very traumatic time for me. She ran away with Rodolfo and then Katie and I drove to Wyoming searching for her and I was afraid we'd lost her forever. But she came back into our lives and I'm very grateful for that.

Sometimes my kids wondered why I spent so much time on civic projects. I told them that "I believe that everyone has an obligation to do a certain amount of volunteer work to improve the world and since a lot of people don't do their share, those of us who believe that must do more than our share." About 1970 our beloved Dr. Krueger was killed in a plane crash and in trying to get another doctor into our community, we had to set up the Ashton Health Services Corporation. I suddenly found myself to be the corporation president and spent the next four or five years trying to get a doctor into the community on a full time basis. I put up the $4500 seed money (I got it back) to build a clinic to encourage doctors to stay in the community. It was used for awhile for the CD (Chemical Dependency) and now for the Medical Clinic again, but we finally had to give up our dream of keeping the hospital open (mostly due to ridiculously restrictive federal regulations we couldn't meet) and allow our hospital to become a nursing home.

Some years before that, I became involved in a battle over the proposal to build a high-school near Chester to serve the entire county. I was very opposed to that idea because I believe that a high-school is very important to every community to give that community a sense of identity and of pride in itself, and also because I believe that students in a small school have many important opportunities that students in a large school do not have. I once debated that issue publicly in the high school auditorium with Markley Case. We had a difficult time trying to fight the larger populated area (St. Anthony) and finally decided that we would attempt to divide the school district. When we found that there was no provision in Idaho law for dividing a school district, a group of us went to Boise to meet with the Joint House-Senate Education Committee. I had expected an informal hearing, but it was very formal and when they asked for our spokesman, I looked around and found that everyone was looking at me so I gave an impassioned impromptu speech and they changed the law. We were able to get the proposed division of the district on the ballot but lost the election, but by then the opposition had given up and we kept our high school.

About 1949 Ricks College decided to become a four year school, so I enrolled and commuted to Rexburg by Greyhound Bus every day for two years and continued to work at Lyon's store every afternoon. They didn't have an engineering college so I majored in Math, and finally graduated with a B.S. in Math with minors in both Chemistry and Physics, because of the courses I had taken at Lehigh U. and at the University of Idaho. Shortly after my graduation, my math professor came to our house and asked me to accompany him to Seattle to work for Boeing as a mathematician. It was a hard decision (sounded like a really neat job) but Katie and I finally decided that we should stay in Ashton, because of extended family ties and quality of life. Then the local high school asked me to teach a half day—one hour each of Algebra, Geometry, and Chemistry. It was really difficult for me to do that and still do the work in the store that needed to be done. Algebra was a snap, but it had been ten years since I had studied Geometry or Chemistry and sometimes I had trouble keeping ahead of the kids. It was a great experience but when the school asked me back (but only if I would take education courses all summer) I decided it had been too hard, and in the meantime business at the store had fallen off to about half of normal so I went back to work at the store full time. There are a couple of ex-students

Newspaper photo of young Glade with phonograph records at Ashton Mercantile

that still call me "Prof." About that time Mrs. Howe hired me to tutor her daughter Margaret in algebra. Now she's the math teacher in the High School.

Along about that time I changed the name of the store from Ashton Mercantile to Lyon's when a little girl came in and asked where Lyon's Store was. Her mother had told her to go to Lyon's to buy something but she couldn't find Lyon's. I tried to meet the needs of the community in the merchandise we carried for sale.

Right after World War II, we bought anything and everything we could for resale. All the major appliances we could because they had been so scarce and because all the returning servicemen were getting married and needed them. We actually had a waiting list for any major appliances we could get. Dad had arranged for a Maytag franchise and I was able to get the franchise to sell RCA Victor and their accompanying lines. We sold large and small appliances, furniture, floor coverings, pots and pans, clothing and shoes for the whole family, phonograph records, and all sorts of household needs. Our basement toyland at Christmas was a major attraction for the kids of Ashton. In our first years in the store, salesmen would call on us frequently and we would buy our goods from them, but as time went on we found that we could do our buying better if we went to Salt Lake to the wholesale houses or to the markets which were held two or three times a year. We got so we knew every cafe in Salt Lake City. We found that Christensen Wholesale in Lehi, Utah, was a good source for many of the things we needed and we bought from them regularly. About five years before we closed the store a salesman from Cotter and Co. out of Chicago came in and we signed up with them to be a V & S Variety store and then were able to buy for lower prices and be more competitive with stores like K-Mart. Then we had to go to Chicago to market twice a year and that was kind of fun and different but really hard work because we would spend from 7 A.M. until 9 P.M. every day for three days trying to decide what to buy from the more than 1,500 manufacturers represented there. For awhile after the name change to Lyon's, I identified our store by painting the name "Lyon's" in large red script on a yellow background on the front of the building. We also had paper bags and wrapping paper with "Lyon's" in red script on a yellow background with red dots scattered around on it. Then later I used plywood to cut out and paint a male lion (with blue eyes) and a female (with brown eyes) and a cub (with blue eyes to signify Kathy, our only child

Lyon's store

at home at the time) and put them on the front of the building. They are now fastened to the side of the barn at the Point.

As soon as TV was being broadcast in the area (about 1951), I began selling TV sets in Lyon's store. Business was good and for a while I carried several brands, but when someone asked me which brand I liked best and I told him RCA, I decided it was dumb to try to sell a brand I felt to be inferior, so I cut back to RCA only. I sold, delivered, and repaired them. I also sold and installed antennas (I quit doing that right after I almost fell off the roof of a three-story

The Point

On July 4, Legionnaires march in front of Lyon's store with its new sign. Glade's handwriting at the bottom

house). Katie and I owned the first color TV set in Ashton and for some years after we got it our living room was full of Murdochs and anyone else on New Year's Day, watching the Rose Parade in ever-living color. Katie made hot cakes for everyone.

The Point

About 1960, Uncle Tom Murdoch bought about seven acres of land on Fall River from Jay Hill. He asked me to come help him lay out square corners for the cabin he wanted to build, and I did. Then a short time later he invited me to watch the foundation being poured. When I got there, they were doing it in a totally different area than we had laid it out (I built a sign for his mantel that said "Uncle Tom's Cabin"), so I asked him to sell me the acre or so where we had originally laid out the rectangle

The Lyon home had the best TV reception in town

for the foundation. It was covered with weeds and sagebrush and cockle-burrs and thistle and wild rose bushes and hawthorne bushes and stinging nettle and chokecherries and a few black willows. We cut weeds and grubbed sagebrush and planted lots of trees and now it is our picnic ground. When we first told people about it, they would ask what piece of ground we were talking about and we would tell them it was that little point of ground where Conant Creek empties into Fall River. And so it became "The Point." When I learned that our ground did not extend to the bank of Conant Creek I got Oberhanslys to sell us half an acre so that we would own both sides of the creek. Later, Martin Bergman showed me that his daughter Eileen Calonge owned some ground at the confluence of the two streams, and I bought that from her. For the first few years we tried to water it from a ditch that Tom and I dug but we weren't very successful. Right after we dug the ditch, Uncle Howard looked at it and said he'd drink every drop that came down it. But when I made a little waterfall and invited him to lie under it with his mouth open, he backed down. After Darrell built his house on top of the ditch we tried to water out of the creek with a little gas-operated pump but that wasn't too successful either. I finally decided to put in electricity, whether we could afford it our not, so we could have a real watering system and really grow trees and grass. The Point has been a major part of our lives and a labor of love. But when people tell me how blessed we are to have such a beautiful place, I like to tell them that they should have seen it when the Lord had it all to himself.

One of the focal points of the Point is the "church rock" that says "1909 Farnum Ward LDS." When Katie first saw it at Dick Egbert's house, she told me she didn't covet much but she did covet that. It was originally over the doorway of the Farnum Ward church that her father built while he was Bishop of the Farnum Ward. When I sold Dick's house for him, he said he didn't want it and the Drummonds, the new owners, didn't either, so Dick brought it to the Point for us.

The "church rock" at the Point

In 1994 Wayne Oberhansley decided to sell the acreage adjoining the Point on the east. The survey showed the Section Line to be about 100 feet east of the fence that everyone had thought was the Section Line. So Jay Hill, our bishop, claimed that he owned that 100 foot wide strip north from the Squirrel Road to the east-west section line near where Conant Creek empties into Fall River and offered to sell it to me for $9,000. After spending more than a couple of thousand dollars on surveyors and attorneys we negotiated with Wayne (Jay Hill had no real claim) and have now established our property line at about the middle of the creek. Not as much property as we should have (we once owned both banks of the creek) but, I guess, acceptable. I (as a real estate agent) sold the 25 acres east of Conant Creek to Eric Adema for about $107,000 in 1997.

Farnum Ward building with the "church rock" over the doorway

Family Vacations

About 1962, I was going through some pictures and suddenly realized that they were of a trip to California we had taken in 1958 and that we had been "nowhere" since then. I told Katie that we were not going to live our lives like that and that I wanted our kids to know that there was a whole world out there to be explored, so we bought a 12 1/2 foot trailer (all we could afford) and took off for the Seattle World's Fair. We had a great time camping on the beach at Beard's Hollow (near the southern tip of Washington) and digging razor clams there, and I made the kids eat snails at the French restaurant and go to a Gilbert and Sullivan operetta. The next year we went to Newport, Oregon (staying at the Waves Motel), then the next year to Disneyland, then to Newport again. We loved hunting for agates on the Oregon beaches. Each year we would take our vacation during "Potato Harvest Vacation" while

Glade and Katie in Oregon, November 1967

the kids were out of school and business was slow at the store. We made many other trips; to San Francisco (we picked up Connie and Ralph and their kids on the way and David became one of the only kids in the world to relieve himself off the Golden Gate Bridge), to Minnesota (while Connie and Ralph lived there), to Kansas to visit my Dad's relatives, to Phoenix with Connie and Ralph (Mom was there on her mission), and wherever we could. Some of the best times of my life.

Robin hunting agates at the beach

Businesses

I remember that about 1963 Jimmie Allison came and sat in my upstairs office at Lyon's and wondered how he could buy the IGA grocery store. So he and I became partners, using my credit. We ran it for seven years while we paid off the major loan and then he bought me out. We had a good relationship and became good friends. Sadly, he was killed in a snowmobile accident about

Gloy and Sarah at work in Lyon's store

1972. His mother, Sarah, worked for me at Lyon's for many years, and I'm sure she loved me at least as much as I loved her.

Jimmie had a connection with someone near the Mexican border so we opened a "Mexican" store in the western room of the theater, and brought in all sorts of Mexican pottery. It did pretty well for a couple of years and gave the kids a place to work.

It was during the time Jimmie and I were partners in the IGA that Clair bought his 1964 Thunderbird. It was the fastest and best driving car I ever saw. Once when I was driving it I had it to 140 miles per hour (the last peg on the speedometer) and when I pressed down on the accelerator I could still feel it move out.

I guess it was in the fifties that I bought a used Ski-doo snowmobile for $300 and then had a lot of fun going with Jimmie and Clair Allison and Darrell Richey and whoever to West Yellowstone and the Centennials and Cave Falls and the Flagg Ranch and wherever. It was a lot of fun and I loved the winter scenery but it was also expensive. It seemed to me that it cost me $50 for repairs

Amphicat

after every trip, so I finally sold it. I bought an "Amphicat" one time thinking I would become a dealer. It had six balloon tires and would go about anywhere. I used it a few times for a golf cart. It would go across a pond as easily as it went on the fairway, but after the gears went out I gave up and sold it.

I always enjoyed collecting coins. I brought a lot of foreign coins home from Europe and Asia and then started collecting pennies. I often would go to the bank and buy a bag of $50 worth of pennies and in the evening I'd go through them and pick out the ones that were the most valuable because of their dates, and then roll the rest and return them to the bank. One summer I took the kids to Fullmer's Beach west of St. Anthony for swimming lessons and on the way I'd stop at the bank and buy a $1,000 bag of silver dollars and while the kids swam I'd look through them and keep out the ones that were worth $5 or more each

The Orange Mart, many years later

according to Coin World. I would usually find about 200 dollars worth keeping. I bought and traded for lots of coins and acquired a pretty nice collection including some gold coins. I even traded for a $3 bill signed by Joseph Smith and Sidney Rigdon. And for a $5 Mormon gold piece which turned out be a fake.

In 1972 I found out that the Orange Mart in St. Anthony was for sale, so I bought it, partly because I had been wondering how I was going to be able to pay for my kids' college. I sold most of my U. S. coin collection for $4,545 to get the down payment and I owned and operated it for twelve years. When I bought it, they bragged that they were doing $100,000 a year. Our third year, we did $315,000. We made some money for about eight years and then started losing. Someone was stealing and I couldn't figure out who it was so I in 1984 I sold it to two young men from the east coast and got it back in about two years (they still owe me a bunch of money). I decided not to try to re-open it and later sold it to a young Mexican man, Manuel Benitez. After two or three years, he quit paying his payments and I had to foreclose, and in 1996 I helped Temo and Bertha Moreno buy it.

Along there somewhere (probably about 1965) Jim Barrett

came to the IGA with a plan for us to use Benny Bee (later changed to Blue Bond) trading stamps as a merchandising promotion. I had been thinking about trying to start a stamp program (S&H Green stamps and Gold Bond stamps were going wild) for the town of Ashton to encourage people to shop at home, so we started with him instead. The stores gave one stamp for each dollar spent when people bought their groceries or other items and the customers would fill small books with the stamps and redeem them for merchandise. It seemed that most people redeemed their stamps at Lyon's for small appliances. A year or so later, Jim introduced me to George Gregersen, who had a brokerage firm in Salt Lake City. I got my Securities License and began selling penny stocks (anything under $3.00 per share) on the OTC (Over-the-Counter) market. We sold new issues almost exclusively, and for a few years everything we sold made money. Then, about 1973, the market crashed and put us out of business but it was sure fun while it lasted.

 Later, I told George he should buy an almost defunct business newspaper in Salt Lake, which he did and renamed the Enterprise and turned it into a really fine and profitable business newspaper. A few years later he thought that he could start other similar newspapers in other cities around the west. Jim Barrett and I and others, invested in, and started, a newspaper in Phoenix. Jim and I were invited to go to Phoenix for a week and help "start the paper" (read "sell advertising"). The first afternoon we got there, we found that the four professional advertising sales teams had started that morning and had left us the worst territory, but we went out and sold two advertising contracts. The last buyer said "you guys are some hellacious salesmen." It turned out that we had made the only sales of the day. It was so funny to see that we had skunked the professional sales teams. The next day I sold the back page, which was what everyone else wanted to do. The paper lasted a couple of years and then went broke, as did the ones in San Diego and San Francisco. I thought I was

Robin, Suzanne, Jack, and Kathy being silly, about 1970

going to become a millionaire, but instead I lost about $70,000. Dumb? Well, perhaps, but you can't win if you don't enter. About the last real contact I had with George was when he called me and reminded me that I was holding a bunch of stock in his corporation that I really didn't own and told me that if I would send him the $25,000 it was worth, he would probably make me a bunch of money and in any case he would "hold me harmless." I believed him so I sent him the money but that was the end of it. That is included in the $70,000 I mentioned before. When Jim Barrett found out that I was probably going to make a bunch of money on the stock he said he wanted in and would pay me half of the $25,000. I said okay but I never got his half either. If it concerns money, don't believe anybody.

Travel

About 1965 I sold enough RCA products to earn a free trip to Europe. Katie and I flew to Maryland and visited Wallace and Pauline for a few days and then met the rest of the tour group in Washington D.C. We then flew to London for three days of castles and sightseeing, like Windsor Castle, Piccadilly Circus, Trafalgar Square, and Westminster Abbey. I wanted to see what a small town in England was like, so Katie and I took a train to Great Missenden and wandered around for most of a day visiting with the shopkeepers. It was so interesting to see the differences in life styles. We then flew to Paris for three days and enjoyed the Eiffel Tower and the Louvre. Saw the "Mona Lisa" and patted "Winged Victory" on her butt. I bought a beret and a long loaf of bread and was walking down the street when a tourist jumped out of the crowd and took my picture. Guess he thought he had a real Parisien. Then on to Nice for three days on the beach. Only the beach was cobble-rocks. The beach at Cannes was sandy and beautiful. We went to Monte Carlo where I played roulette and left with twenty of their dollars. Then to Madrid for more art galleries and the really interesting "Thieves Market." And then to Lisbon which we liked most of all (we stayed at the Ritz). We took the train to Cas-Cas where we met a little boy with a toy gun on each hip—a real cowboy. Most of this time we spent with Bill and Shirlene Davis from Spanish Fork and became good friends with them. On our return, I insisted that Katie see New York City so we stopped over for a couple of days and did all the tourist things, then on home.

Property

In 1964 we decided to find a piece of ground out of town and build a new home on it. We finally found the piece we wanted, sixteen acres east of Don Marshall, but when the owner wouldn't sell it, we decided to add on to our home. I had planned to do most of the work myself but decided that I was too busy at the store so I had John Marsden add the garage, the new living room, a basement room, and two bedrooms and a bath over the garage for about $16,000. We later bought that sixteen acres from the Murray Baum estate for $20,000 and a year later sold four acres and the house Murray had moved onto it for $23,000, leaving us with about twelve acres (that we call the North Eleven) at no cost to us (after commissions, etc.), but by then Katie had decided that she no longer wanted to live out of town.

About that time I went in with Arlen Mortensen and some others on a land deal just north of St. Anthony. Over a few years I got back my original $10,000 investment plus a five acre lot on the west bank of the Ashton Reservoir which we called the "West Five." After a few years I sold that to Gary Beardall on a time payment contract for $25,000.

About 1963 Jim Harrell asked me to go in with him and a group of about a dozen others and buy the old Carl Reimann place of 560 acres which we renamed "Potpourri Ranch" and proceeded to sell the north 155 acres for $1000 per acre and then subdivide eighty acres of it into lots of two acres or more. I think my original investment was $2,500 and then some other one or two thousand dollar loans to the corporation, but it has paid off handsomely over the years. We originally paid a little less than $250 per acre and the last we sold was for almost $9000 per acre. My biggest mistake was not buying some of the better lots because they are now worth much more than originally.

Mexico

In the early spring of 1972, Katie's brother Wallace invited us to visit him in Mexico City (he was there on business), so to celebrate our 25th wedding anniversary we arranged with J.T. and Lois to take the train to Mexico City with us. It was a laughable disaster. Our compartment was only one-half the size we expected (the four of us shared a compartment with only two narrow beds) and the trip took 24 hours longer than we were told, but we had such a great time that we took the train back to Mexicali (con un comparto doble) rather than fly back as originally planned. We spent about three weeks in and around Mexico City (visited Taxco and the temples of the sun and moon) and loved it. We enjoyed it so much that we talked Jim and Sadie Harrell into going to Mexico with us the next year and many other years. One time we flew into Puerto Vallarta and stayed at a small Mexican hotel near the river. We took a cab up to a cafe that we could see on the hill where we had a couple of Margaritas and then the waiter came out with a tray. At first, I thought it was hors d'oeuvers and then realized it was all raw meat. He said it was the menu and when I asked how much, he said "it doesn't matter." And we found out he was right because the bill for all four of us was only $25.

Perhaps the best vacation we ever had was when the four of us flew into Mexico City, rented a car and drove a thousand miles in about ten days without knowing where we were going. We visited Morelia, Patzquaro, San Juan del Cobre, Uruapan, Leon, Guanajuato, San Miguel de Allende, Queretaro, San Juan del Rio, and Tequisquiapan, plus others. I highly recommend this but suggest you fly into Guadalajara rather than Mexico City because of the Mexico City traffic. Another time we flew into the island of Cozumel, Quintana Roo for a few days and then to Merida, Yucatan where we visited the ruins of Chi-Chen-It-Za and Tulum. Other trips to Mexico included Mazatlan, Guadalajara, and Puerto Vallarta. One year we were in Mazatlan for Carnival and were fascinated by the fabulous floats in the parade. Another great trip was when we took the train from Los Mochis through the Copper Canyon and stayed at Margaritas's in Creel (home of the Tarahumara Indians) for a couple of days. That was in 1991 when we went with Jim and Sadie Harrell and Cal and Ruth Wickham and two other couples to Etzatlan, a small town about an hour west of Gudalajara. There were two motor homes, two fifth-wheels and us po' folk in our 23' trailer. Carnival was on while we were there and it was great. We went to the bull fights and the chareadas (rodeos) and the parades and the crowning of the king and queen. We were asked to (and did) help sponsor the refreshments for one of the days of Carnival. That is, one of the days that you could have all the free tequila and Squirt you wanted to drink, in the plaza. We met two teen-age sisters; Lucy, who wanted to learn English (she came out to our trailer and we gave her lessons), and Regina, who wanted to be queen of her class (we helped her collect money so she could win, but she didn't). Then we went to La Penita and nearby Puerto Vallarta and had fun on the beach for awhile, and finally home after 46 days in Mexico. And we visited Cosala and Grandma Celia (Rodolfo's mother) in nearby Palo Verde. What a fantastic vacation.

Bowling

I had been bowling as the captain of "Lyon's" team at the alley in St. Anthony, but when Joe Rankin started Pine Bowl in Ashton we started bowling there. Katie and I both had a lot of fun bowling in mixed leagues for several years. I usually averaged about 175. My high line was 259 and Katie's was 222. We bowled as a team with Richard and Erna Reinke one summer in Rexburg.

Church

About 1960 Mother was called on a mission and was ready to go when she broke her wrist and had to postpone it for a year. She so badly wanted me to become active in the church that I agreed to take some lessons, and so for some months we met with Bob Archibald and some other couples in our living room once a week and studied the gospel. After a year I was ordained an elder and Katie and I were married in the temple and had our kids sealed to us. I accepted the job as Stake Secretary of the Aaronic Priesthood although I thought it was a mistake (I should have been going to classes with my peers). I did the job and kept the attendance records, which I thought were totally useless and just make-work, for awhile, and then they released me from that and made me the Sunday School Superintendent. I chose Clair Allison and Hugh Hammond for my counselors and I think we did a good job for about four years. There are some teachings in the church that I don't agree with, but I do believe that having children attend Sunday School and teaching them morals and values is very important. When Jack was blessed, I stood in the circle and participated, but when Suzanne was blessed they said that since I was not an elder I could not participate—the rules had been changed (part of the unchanging principles of the gospel). Just at that time I was asked to speak in Stake Conference (just prior to being made an elder), so I gave a bitter speech that pointed out scriptures that gave the father the right to stand in that circle. There was a general authority present and I expected I would be excommunicated but instead they changed the rule back (see above: unchanging principles). One day, both HughB and Clair told me they would not be present at Sunday School the next week (they were going hunting) and I bet them each $5 that they would be. They gleefully took the bet, and then I asked each of them to stand in the circle for Suzanne's confirmation that next Sunday. I collected the $5 from each of them.

Glade, Katie, and kids on the grounds of the Mesa Temple during Gloy's mission to Arizona

Ashton Ward building, directly across the street from Glade and Katie's home in Ashton

Fun

I've always liked to play games. Pinochle was the favorite game of most everyone in Tetonia and my folks would have pinochle parties at our home and invite several couples to play. I remember when I was about ten, when Mom went to fix refreshments, I would sit in and play her hand. I don't suppose the other adults liked it, but I thought I was as good as anyone. After Katie and I were married, we had lots of pinochle parties. We'd invite about five couples so we could play three tables, and we'd play eight games of four hands to a game and then have refreshments and check scores to see who had won the inexpensive prizes. We've played about a million games of pinochle with Velda and Noel, either at our homes or out in the desert after a long day of sage hen hunting. I was ten when the game of Monopoly was first brought out. I really wanted one but didn't have the $2.99 it probably cost, and my folks wouldn't buy me one, so I borrowed one and copied the whole thing; the board, the property cards, the chance cards, the opportunity cards—everything. Sure wish I still had that homemade game.

Two of my priorities when I went to college were to learn to play chess and to learn to play golf. One of my college friends taught me to play chess. Golf was a Physical Education course I could take for credit, so that was automatic. And I loved them both. When someone tells me they don't play golf, I like to say "you mean to tell me you've just wasted your whole life"? But I probably wasted too much of my life on the game. The most frustrating game there is. And the most fun. I helped start the Fremont County Golf Course by donating $100 to help get enough money to buy the ground and then spent some time there with a shovel and a rake actually helping to build it. I played in some leagues but really enjoyed just playing with my buddies more than that. I never was very good (my handicap usually not less that 15) but really enjoyed playing. I liked to play in tournaments and one year I played in the Idaho State Amateur in Idaho Falls and took third place in the seventh flight. Wow!

Earl Jensen from Preston (another RCA dealer) owned his own plane and for several years, he (and sometimes his brother) would fly up and get me and one of my friends and we would fly to Jackson Hole or Sun Valley or Twin Falls and play a round of golf and then fly home. They were all really great trips.

In the army, three of my friends and I played pinochle until one of them and I said the other two would have to learn to play bridge because we were sick of pinochle. They protested but finally agreed to try it and then we couldn't ever get them to play pinochle again. The two of us thought we were really good bridge players so on the way from the Philippines to Japan we went around challenging everyone to a game for a tenth of a cent a point. We finally found two suckers who would play us and we lost fifty dollars each so quick we hardly knew what happened.

Sickness

I've been really sick a couple of times and probably should mention it. I had amoebiasis about 1962, and always thought I got it from the clams we dug at Beard's Hollow, Washington (or the filthy place we cleaned them) on our way to the Seattle World's Fair. And about ten years later I got "Q" fever. I think I caught it from HughB although the doc said you only got it from cows. Anyway, Dr. Krueger told me he thought that's what I had and he'd send a blood sample to Montana for confirmation. He said I'd either be dead or cured by the time we found out if I had it. That first night (before I went to the doctor) I had chills and fever all night but when morning came I felt a lot better but then when I took my temperature it was 105. Wonder how high it was when I was really sick? They wanted to hospitalize me but I wouldn't go, so I spent a month in bed at home. I remember trying to walk to the store after about 30 days. I was so weak that after a block and a half I almost turned around. But I kept on and finally made it. I did let Dr. Krueger talk me into a hernia operation about 1960. Sixty days later I tore it out (when I picked up a washing machine my two teen age helpers couldn't move) and it needs to be done again but it's only been about forty years so I think I'll wait awhile.

Hunting

I think it was in 1972 that Velda and Noel and Katie and I went sage hen hunting together for the first time. They had a camper on the back of their pick-up and we all slept in it and used the canvas sided outhouse that Noel built. The next year we'd bought our first Blazer so opening morning (always the third Saturday in September) we took off for the Split Butte area. We really didn't know where to go but after awhile Katie said to turn on that road (the one we were on was really dusty) and she sounded like she meant it, so I did. We had gone about a mile when we saw two sage hens in the road. By the time Noel got his shotgun put together there were six. We shot them and then realized that we had filled our limits (Velda didn't have a license) so we'd have to go home. Instead, I suggested we go up the Sadorus Hill Road and look for a ruffed grouse. We found some blue grouse instead along the road and shot six of them. Decided to clean them there and then later found, to our consternation, that we had seven gizzards and that has always been a major puzzlement because sage grouse don't have gizzards. We never have figured that one out. We kept on going each year, taking our trailer and the Hill's 5th wheel and camping in different locations, mostly on Camas Creek. Some of the best times of our lives.

More Business Ventures

When I got out of the service I looked around for an easy way to make money. Slot machines were illegal but Idaho law enforcement was looking the other way, so I bought four slot machines and a couple of pinball machines and put them in locations that the local mafia (slot machine kings) didn't want to bother with. I put them in service stations and small cafes. They made money and things were going well until the state decided to make them legal and put a $500 per machine license on them. That put me out of business because that was about what I was making on each one of them.

Several years later Jimmie Allison, Clair Allison, Hugh Hammond, Louis Smith, Darrell Richey, Ted Stronks, and their wives, and Katie and I decided to buy the local Ashton Theater because it was so run down and we thought the town needed a theater. I was president of the corporation that we formed and Clair was secretary-treasurer. We hoped to make some money, but that never happened. But we cleaned it and painted it and repaired the seats and finally opened up with the movie "It's a Mad, Mad, Mad, Mad,

World." We had a cafe on the corner but it lost money. We found that the leased pinball machines were making good money so we bought three of our own, using my contacts from my slot machine days. The pinballs did so well that we ended up with about a hundred of them and Clair and I, and sometimes Jimmie, ran routes to West Yellowstone, to Victor, and to Rigby, putting them in cafes for the most part. We did okay for awhile, but Clair got tired of running the place and I got tired of helping him, and the others never helped much so we finally sold out.

Travel

One summer, Ralph had to give a lecture in Lethbridge, Canada, so we tied on to our travel trailer and went with them. I remember that when we came out of Canada our dog "Buster Keaton" was sitting in the front seat and the guards asked for his papers. I said we didn't have any and they wanted to know how we got him into Canada. They said we would have to leave him but when I said okay, but they'd have to take the kids as well, they backed off. It was a great trip and we took in Glacier Park and Waterton Lakes Park in Canada as well as Lake Louise. I remember traveling south of Banff and Jasper Parks; Ralph was in the lead, and when I turned on my lights (our signal to stop) he came back and asked what was the matter. I waved in utter amazement at the snow covered mountain range on each side of the valley we were traveling through, and he said "just another fantastically beautiful mountain range."

Pets

Pets were a big part of our life as our kids grew up. We had cats; a big orange one named Champagne and a big black one named Dover (short for Lover-Dover) that would ride around the kids necks like a fur piece or would lay on the TV and swat at

Robin with Dover

the images as they moved by. We had dogs; Old Yeller, Buttons, Buster Keaton, Honey Pot, Fido, and a stray we named Happy that everyone[3] loved. When the City of Ashton passed an ordinance that required all dogs to be kept on a leash, I took ours up to the City and had them euthanized. I've been extremely sorry ever since and I don't think the kids ever forgave me. One of the biggest mistakes of my life.

We had fish; at least 2000 guppies at one time in a big tank in the basement, and we had AC, a mynah bird (my grandfather's name was A. C. Miner) that we had for about 23 years, that would scream "Hello" when the phone rang, "Hi" when the door bell rang, or "What's Your Name?" when someone walked up to his cage. Once Katie insisted, so we sold him to the Pet Shop, but in a month or two she made me buy him back. We also had the usual assortment of small animals, wild and domestic, like mice, chipmunks, hamsters, rabbits, ducks, etc. But now we only have Salli and Mandi; mud-puppies (salamanders) that live in a hole in the concrete at the bottom of the steps to my basement workshop. I feed them a nightcrawler now and then. And Katie keeps a supply of wild bird seed on the deck for the birds she loves to watch.

Hunting and Camping

Although I was never very good, I enjoyed shooting a bow and arrow. I was instrumental in setting up a "Field Archery Course" on the Ashton hill and was president of the club we formed. There were 14 targets ranging from 15 feet to 75 yards and we shot three arrows at each one and kept our scores and had a lot of fun. Hunting, I shot at a couple of deer and a couple of elk and they hardly noticed. I did once shoot the head off a ruffed grouse. One of the best hunting trips I ever had was hunting alone with

---

3. Except Jack.

Jack with Buttons

Lyon home with Happy on front porch

a bow up by Bear Gulch. I stalked two deer for several hours. They just played with me. Whenever I was close enough for a shot there was brush between us. When it was clear, they were too far away. I never took a shot but it was a great day. Once when the blue-back salmon were in their spawning run (they turned bright red) in Lucky Dog Creek in Island Park, we tried to shoot them with fish-arrows. It was fun but I don't think we ever hit one.

Once, early in the spring, I took Jeff Hemming with me to see if the snow was gone enough so we could get to the archery course.

Just after we turned off the highway, we jumped a yearling moose. He ran up the road we were going on so I followed right on his heels. As we came to the top of the hill, he pulled off to the left and stopped. I pulled up even with him and sat there about five feet from him. We looked at each other for a while until finally, he backed up a few steps, put his head down and charged the car. At the last second, he changed course enough to miss us except to hit his leg on the front bumper with a loud clang. He ran up ahead and came back across to the left side of the road again and I pulled up, but just as I got to him, he charged again, but this time he veered off and missed us entirely and we didn't see him again. I always said that at the last minute, he remembered how bad it had hurt the first time.

The first deer I ever shot was out in the sagebrush desert west of Ashton about 1947. I had Dad's old model 94 Winchester 30–30 (the biggest gun I ever owned), and suddenly a deer was walking past me about a hundred yards away. I shot and it started to run; I shot again and it slowed to a walk; I shot again and it started to run and then I saw it go down. I was surprised that I had apparently missed it twice, but when we dressed it out, we found three ribs that had each been broken by a bullet.

Another story I always liked to tell was when Marv Tighe and I were driving up the dugway just north of the confluence of Rock Creek and Robinson Creek. I looked across the deep canyon to our right and asked him if he'd shoot a deer on the other side if we saw one there and he said "no way" because it'd be too much work to get it out. And of course, right then there was a three point buck and we both jumped out and Marv shot and I shot and Marv shot again, but when I shot the second time the deer jumped up in the air and turned around and started to run and then went down. We went back down to the bridge and parked and found a log to cross on (trying to keep from getting wet) and finally found the deer and dressed it (it had one bullet right through the heart) and started back but the brush was so thick that we finally let it roll down into the creek and we followed it and each grabbed an antler and waded down the creek pulling it behind us. It was November and there was four inches of snow on the ground and it was cold!

Once when Marv and I were goose hunting just below Fritz bridge, I knocked one down in the middle of the river. We tried to get it out but couldn't, so Marv showed me how to get to the Chester Dam and I waded out in the river up to my armpits. Sure was wet and cold, but I got the goose. Now that's dumb.

Hugh Hammond and I were driving on a dim road up-stream from Upper Mesa Falls when a bunch of deer started running alongside us. We both jumped out and Hugh started shooting but I waited until the big buck stopped about 150 yards away and looked back. I shot him in the neck. We dressed him and put him in Hugh's garage. Later Hugh got a cow elk and hung it by the deer. They looked the same size so Hugh took them both down to Jimmie Allison at IGA and weighed them. He said the deer weighed 300 and the elk was 306. Later both Tom Murdoch and Russell Rammell said that deer don't get that big, but Hugh says he doesn't care what they say, he knows how much they weighed. In the meantime, Jimmie got killed in a snowmobile accident, so he couldn't verify the weight. I thought the a-typical antlers were really neat so I kept them.

I remember once when John Davidson and Larry Smith and I were hunting in John's Jeep, coming down off High Point at about forty miles an hour when suddenly there were two elk running along-side us on the left. John slammed on the brakes and they crossed the road in front of us. I was in the middle, and we all piled out but I was the only one that took a shot. The big bull went down and a cloud of dust came up, but when we ran up there, he'd gotten up and disappeared. Maybe I just hit him in the antlers.

Bob Bean and his boys and I went deer hunting up around High Point once and found some deer just off the road. Bob and his boys had each shot their deer when there suddenly appeared one right near me. They hollered "shoot it" so I shot and it disappeared and then suddenly reappeared (I couldn't believe I'd missed) so I shot again. When I got over to it, there were two, one on top of another. Just then Marv Tighe came along with a guy we didn't know and checked out our kill but didn't notice (and we didn't dare explain) that we had one too many. We went back that night and got the extra one.

The first time I applied for an antelope permit I got it, so Bob Bean and Katie and I went over near Mud Lake and went out into a hay field after dark and climbed on a hay stack and went to sleep. Soon after we awoke we saw two antelope grazing about 400 yards away. After a little while they got nervous and started to run. I tried shooting in front of them and suddenly they started to run right toward us (at 60 miles an hour). I'd fired all my shells and the rest were in a box in my pocket. I finally got my gloves off and got one shell in the chamber of my Model 94 Winchester 30.30 and shot one. It was sure exciting.

A few years later, John Davidson and Helen and Katie and I each put in for an antelope and we all drew. We took John's Jeep and four rifles and two boxes of ammunition for each rifle and went to a campsite southeast of Gilmore. At the end of the first day's hunt we had one antelope and were out of ammo. We went to town and got more and the next day managed to get the other three. One was a big buck and I still have his horns. We even got our pictures, with our four antelope, in the Salt Lake Tribune.

Then Helen Davidson drew a moose permit (three day hunt) for the area east of Last Chance. She and John and I hunted for two days and then Helen gave out but John and I went back the third day. We stopped at Last Chance for gas and the Kuck kid gave us a bad time about we couldn't find a moose and we couldn't hit it if we did find one and my little 30.06 rifle wouldn't kill one anyway. I told him we'd find one and I'd shoot it in the eye, in the *right eye,* and bring it back to show him. About eight hours later, there was a cow moose about 75 yards in front of me, looking at me. I tried to get John to shoot it but he could only see its hind quarters and it was looking straight at me, so I aimed right between the eyes and pulled off just enough to hit it in the right eye. The kid couldn't believe that there wasn't another hole in it somewhere, but there wasn't.

I was never a really avid hunter like Noel and some of my other friends, but I went when I could and usually enjoyed it. Unless it was too cold or too early in the morning. I think I already said that the two things I hate the most are going to bed and getting up. Especially getting up. Especially early. Like right now it is 1:30 A.M. and I'm just getting going. I remember once when I went into Laurel's Cafe for breakfast about 7:30 in the morning (really early) and asked where all the hunters were. Laurel laughed at me and said they had all gone hours before and there was no sense in my even going out so late. I told him the deer were out there all day long. I went up on Blue Creek and saw some deer sign, walked up the creek for a while and then back and sat down on the edge of the cliff overlooking the creek for a few minutes when a doe walked out of the willows and into the edge of the timber and just as I was ready to shoot, a three point buck followed her out. I shot him and was back in town in a couple of hours and took him to show Laurel Huntsman, the cook.

Some of us used to go pheasant hunting over around Monteview and that was lots of fun, but after a few years the bird population was way down and we quit that. I remember one time I got out of the car and jumped over a ditch and came down with my left foot on something soft that went "phffft." The weeds were up to my chin and I couldn't see what it was but when I moved my foot it ran and then flew. It was a rooster pheasant and I got it.

I liked to hunt ducks, especially walking up Willow Creek in Putney canyon north of town. When the ducks jumped up you might get a shot but since the canyon got really narrow, in just a few minutes they'd be back and you'd get another shot at them. I once got three ducks in three shots, which was pretty unusual for me. I'll never forget the time Steve Durst and I hunted along Sewer Creek by Baker's and when we came to an electric fence and I very carefully tried to straddle it, he laughed at me. He, with his long legs, straddled it with no problem at all until his gun barrel hit the hot wire.

    I was about 55 years old when Noel told me that he and Blake were going on a hike up in the Tetons. He said they planned to take a week to hike about 35 miles. I was playing lots of golf at the time and since it's about five miles around a golf course, I figured it wouldn't be too bad so I begged to go with them and they let me. The gals took us up near Grassy Lake and I put my 50 pound pack on my back and we headed south. We got a little lost but ended up on Berry Creek as originally planned and camped there. We had some Soup-Starter and built a fire and found out that we were so high up that we couldn't boil the water to cook it. But we were hungry. The next day we hiked on to Owl Creek and up it to a spring where we had planned to spend the next night. But the spring was dry and we hadn't brought enough water so we had to go on to a larger spring. I remember hiking the trail along Owl Creek where the wild bluebells were almost up to my chin and there must have been ten acres of them. Fantastic! I also remember coming to one hill where I told them there was no way in hell I was going to make it up, but I was wrong. I did it one step at a time. We camped at the big spring that night and then went down to Camp Lake the next night. Killed a blue grouse (illegal) and had it and some trout for dinner. Then on to Hidden Corrals for a night where there was a terrible rain and lightning storm. I don't know why, but my heart began to beat so hard I thought I might not make it. But the next day was beautiful and we kept on until we came to North Leigh Creek and down it to the old mill that Noel had worked around and found a truck that we hot-wired and drove to Tetonia in. We hiked forty-four miles in five days. It was one of the real highlights of my life. If you haven't done it, get started.

Another great time I had was when Junior Atchley invited me to go with him on horseback into the Bechler country. I'd never ridden a horse in my life, but I went and it was great. We camped on Boundary Creek and the next day we rode up to Iris Falls and Colonnade Falls. They were breathtaking. It was a great trip. You should have seen me, after I'd lost the stirrups, riding at full gallop across the Bechler Meadows.

Still another great trip was when we and the Andersens went into the Bechler Meadows with all our kids. We had one horse to carry our supplies and hiked in and camped overnight on Boundary Creek. We fished a little on the Bechler River and caught some crayfish on Boundary Creek and had a great time. But we stayed a little too long and when we came out it was dark and the horse was really anxious to go home, so it was quite a trip, carrying bawling kids and trying to slow the horse down.

Teton Dam Disaster

In 1976 the Teton Dam gave way. Katie was in the St. Anthony Hospital recovering from a hysterectomy. Noel and I were playing in a golf tournament at Aspen Acres. We were told the water would be a foot deep in the Orange Mart so we left the tournament and hurried to St. Anthony and moved all the merchandise from the bottom shelves to the top (the water never got there). I spent the next week or two with my daughters and what other help we could get, cleaning up the mud that was left in O. R. Anderson's home and wherever else we were needed. About the third day that we went to help out we had to go way out west because the other roads were closed and we were stopped by the National Guard at the west edge of Rexburg (they were afraid we were looters). So we went to Teton Basin and came back into Rexburg from the north without being stopped and so I went (I was mad) to the man in charge of the National Guard who then gave me a pass to go anywhere I wanted to go. It was a terrible disaster.

Lyon and Andersen kids, about 1963: Jack, Suzanne, Sallie, Robin, David, Steven, Kathy

Foreign Friends

One night as I was on my way home from a Legion conference in Indianapolis, I picked up a young hitchhiker in Pocatello and when I got to the Orange Mart I called Katie and told her to fix us some supper. When she got through berating me for picking up a hitchhiker, I told her to fix the spare bed too. She was really mad at me but three days later when Paul Bos from Holland was ready to leave, she gave him a hug. A couple of years later his sister Louise came and spent a week with us.

Driving from Salt Lake City one day, we came up behind a car with a sign on the rear which said "We are French, help us discover America." We invited the Genot family (Marcel and Josette and four kids) to visit us, which they did, and we took them to the Point for a picnic where all the kids had to hold the water snake we caught and have their picture taken with it. Then a few years later, in 1997, Marcel and Josette came again and stayed with us for a couple of days. They called on New Year's Day 1998 and again invited us to visit them.[4]

Real Estate

About 1978 Jim Harrell finally convinced me I should get my Real Estate Salesman's license and work for him. I didn't think I wanted to, but it has been a great job and a great experience. I enjoy visiting with people and showing property to them and making an occasional sale and when I do the commissions are nice.

In 1989, the year after we closed Lyon's store, the Chamber of Commerce honored Katie and me by choosing us as the Grand Marshals for the fourth of July parade. We rode in a horse drawn buggy and waved to our friends. What an honor.

Perhaps around 1985 I decided to give my wife and each of my

---

4. In 2003, Jack and daughter Rachel stayed several days with the Genot family in Nancy, France.

daughters a pair of heart-shaped earrings for Valentine's Day. I've been doing it ever since, except it has grown. I'm giving eighteen pair this year of 1998 to some of my female relatives, and a heart shaped ring to each of the three two-year-olds.

About 1993, I, as a real estate agent, sold 24 acres of ground just north of Ashton's Visitor Center to Corwin Coughlin from Bozeman, Montana and he (and his buddy, Steve Lemon) built a Super 8 Motel and a convenience store and a restaurant there. They named the restaurant "Glade's Family Restaurant" after me because they said I had helped them so much. That's neat. Now, in 1998 they have changed to "Burger King" and are going to give me the sign "Glade's Family Restaurant." Wonder what I should do with it.

Family Reunion

In 1994 I rented enough rooms in the Gitche Gumee Motel at Oceans Shores on the southern Washington coast (it cost me $1000) for all of the Lyon family and we held our three day reunion there. It was really fun. The kids had asked a lot of our friends to write a letter about our times with them and it is a really nice book. Being able to use the multi-purpose room for meals and gatherings made it extra nice. Steve took charge of the program when we baptized Katie[5] and Melanie in the ocean.

In 1995 I got permits from the Idaho Water Resources Board and the U. S. Army Corps of Engineers and had Weldon use some big rocks to build a "drop structure" in Conant Creek. I applied for a permit to "decrease the erosion and improve the fishery," and it was granted. I was afraid that if I told them we were building a swimming hole they'd turn us down. Now it is our baptismal font. Leah was baptized there the summer of 1996 and Howard's daughter LaRae had her son baptized there in 1997.

---

5. Anderson (Kathy and Steve's daughter).

Lyon reunion at the Gitche Gumee Motel

Whenever Katie and I went on a trip and found a pretty rock or an unusual rock, we'd bring it home. We put them in a rock garden at the back of the house, but when we built a deck there we took them to the Point. In 1996 I decided to build them into a monument. I took the Fall River Jade rock (that the iceberg carried up a few years earlier when the river froze solid clear to the bottom and then broke it loose and carried it up and left it by the fire pit) and had it cut in half and engraved "Lyon's Point," and then over a period of a couple of weeks or so I, along with some help from Scott and Aaron, took the assorted rocks and mudded them into a "Sheepherder's Monument." When Katie and I were in Lewiston for the State Legion Convention we bought a $100 cement lion to put on top. Out in the sagebrush desert west of Ashton, there are lots of "sheepherder's monuments" where sheepherders have stacked rocks to help them find their way back to camp. Now we have a sheepherder's monument so we can tell where we are.

The winter of 96–97 brought lots of snow and in the spring of '97 we had water a foot deep running over the northern part of the Point. To try to stop that from happening again, I got some used power poles and cut them into more or less six foot lengths and had Scott and Aaron help me make them into a levee (or whatever you want to call it) along the bank of Conant Creek to form a sort of dike to reduce the flow across that area. I fastened them down with some steel rods driven into the ground and hope that'll keep them from floating away.

In February 1997, Katie and I drove to San Bernardino to visit JT and Henrietta (his third wife) for a few days. We played a lot of pinochle and had a good time. He's really lucky to have Henrietta, she's a great gal. Played eighteen holes of golf and he beat me (he's eleven years older than I, so he's had lots more practice). I took a tape recorder and got JT to talk into it for about three hours, about his early life especially. I plan to include it in a book of the life histories of all of the descendants of my grandfather, A.

Monument at the Point, with the "church rock" in the background

C. Miner. I'm not getting much encouragement from my cousins, but I'm still working on it.

Henrietta and JT

In the fall of '97 Jack suggested I write a book about "math for dummies" or something. I've been writing a little, giving some of the basic math ideas that I think are important or helpful for everyone to know but it's pretty slow going. Maybe my grandkids will use it. Maybe it'll never get finished. Probably not.

Computers

I find that I have hardly mentioned computers, and that's weird, since this is done on one. I remember one time when Kathy and Steve were going to BYU and came home for Thanksgiving. I had gone to the high school and taken a first class in programming in BASIC and Kathy was working as a programmer for a company in

Orem so I got Bill Dick at Radio Shack to loan me a computer for the weekend so they could teach me everything. The problem was, we never figured out how to turn it on. Not much later I bought one from Radio Shack (which I later gave to Kathy) and learned to use it a little. Then Suzanne got a grant to buy some for the school and told me I could buy one like them for a good price from El-Gene in Rexburg. That's the one I'm using now. It started out as a 486DX with 4 megs of RAM and a 200 meg hard drive. I've upgraded it a few times but it is still too slow. Perhaps some one some day will be amazed to learn that this computer has a tower with a 5 1/4 inch floppy disc drive and a 3 1/2 inch disc drive and an added 2x CD ROM drive. It has 8 megs of RAM (upgraded from four) and a 1.6 gig hard drive (replacing a 200 meg) and an added one meg sound card and operates at 33 megahertz. I mostly use the word processor (Word Perfect 5.2) in Windows 3.1 and the spreadsheet in Microsoft Works and the check register in Quicken, and send e-mail to friends and family in Eudora, and keep track of my stock portfolio on Yahoo and search the net on MetaCrawler for recipes or information on health problems or whatever. When I was first learning how to operate it, I had a problem so I called Jack and told him I needed help from an expert. He said "have you read the book Dad, they say an expert is somone who has read the book." So I'm still not an expert. But I love using e-mail and using the search engines to get information. I wonder what life will be like fifty years from now. Fifty years ago I didn't even have a television set. I just got the screen saver "Johnny Castaway" showing a little guy living on an island with one palm tree (and one of everything behind it) and I'm fascinated by his antics. It seems there is always something new going on in his life. It blows my mind to think of someone doing all that programming.

In 1996 my eye doctor, Dr. Crandall, said that he saw evidence of macular degeneration and that it was a little worse than it had been previously. Then again in early 1998 he found the disease to be progressing, so I went to Dr. Kirk Winward, a retinal surgeon in Salt Lake City, who told me that I have dry (wet is worse) macular degeneration and that there is no cure, so I am slowly going blind. Damn! I went back to him in the spring of 1999 but he says it is still progressing but there is nothing he can do for me. I'm taking lots of vitamins and minerals and herbs including Lutein in hopes that they will help, but I believe the disease is progressing steadily. The telephone poles along the highway seem to have gotten crooked.

In the spring of 1998, Bill Dick gave me back our old store building (whether I wanted it or not). I've had the roof fixed and the back wall repaired and paid the back taxes and it is now leased to Ann Oldham who is planning on putting in a bakery. But, as of 12/5/1998 she is eight months behind on her rent. I just (January 1999) figured out that we have spent well over $6200 on repairs, back taxes, etc. In March 1999 Bill Bates came to me and wanted to lease the store building for $400 a month with an option to purchase it for $45,000 in 5 years (he paid me $1200 for the option) so we talked to Oldhams and went ahead with Bates. In September he said he was not doing as well as he had hoped and asked to have the rent reduced to $250 per month, so I agreed to that for the next six months only.

A major event in my life was the day of June 17, 1998 when I climbed the extension ladder from our deck to the roof of the house and had just started back down when the feet of the ladder slipped and I rode the ladder to the deck. I broke off two teeth (#9 and #10) above the gum line when I hit the edge of the roof with my mouth and badly bruised my left hip along with other parts of my body, but I could just as easily have broken my neck and been paralyzed forever. Just lucky. My theory is, that if you wake up and then you can get up, that's terrific.

When Ryan returned from his mission, he wanted to enroll in BYU but they wouldn't accept him because his grades at Ricks before he went on his mission had not been good enough. He's been taking some classes over to improve his grades. I think that the church should honor every honorably discharged missionary by allowing him or her to enroll in the college or university of his or her choice, so I wrote a letter to the president of the church telling him that. I received an answer from Henry B. Eyring which didn't say a lot except that there are too many returning missionaries to make it possible. When you see what you consider to be an injustice, do something about it.

Cody is back from his mission in Australia and he has grown both mentally and physically. He's currently (summer 1998) working as a cook at Henry's Fork Landing at Mack's Inn but will go back to Ricks as soon as the fall term starts.

In July of 1998, Katie and I bought a new trailer. A brand new 30 foot Kit with a tip-out and an awning and a furnace and an air conditioner and a queen size bed that you can walk on both sides of (Katie says it's the hardest one she's ever seen) and a couch that makes into a bed and two bunk beds, etc. They said it was over $26,200 but they priced it at $16,725 and then knocked off $3,500 because hail had pitted the aluminum siding and it ended up $13,225 (plus tax). They parked it at the Point for us and I plan to leave it there forever. They told me my Blazer isn't big enough to pull it (my lucky day!). We plan to spend lots of time in it. Too bad, kids, we took it out of your inheritance. We thought about building a cabin but the taxes would be be lots more and the insurance would be prohibitive. Now we've built a shed over it so the snow won't mash it in (final cost of the shed turned out to be $2614).

1999—Ryan is attending BYU, Cody and Matt are both going to Ricks and Rachel is going to City College in Salt Lake. We're sending each of them $50 per month. It's not much, but I guess every little bit helps. We told our grandkids that we would give each one of them $50 per month as long as they were on missions or were enrolled as full time students in college. I also promised each of them a nice ($200 or $300) birthday present on their 12th (later changed to 16th) birthday. I think that Wren, Melanie and

Kathy's kids are the only ones left to collect on that. Ryan, Aaron, Cody, and Scott all got shotguns or rifles, John got a snowboard, Matt a fishing pole, Rebekah and Rachel wanted cash (against my general policy but I did it anyway), Maria got a keyboard and Wren got nothing so far.

I'm worrying about the potential Y2K problem. The worst case scenario is that all the computers will crash when the year 2000 rolls around and all the power grids will go down and all the computers will cease to function. That will mean no power, no water, no gasoline, no banking, etc. The best case scenario is probably a minor "bump in the road." We are stocking some extra food and water and cash and thinking a lot about extra gasoline, etc. If all the power grids go down for a week or two or more, there will be chaos in the cities and perhaps everywhere. We have our little "sheepherder's stove" in the basement ready to install for heat and cooking, and we are starting to store some water. Every time we empty a 2 liter Diet Coke bottle we fill it with water and add a drop of Purex. When we go grocery shopping we usually buy a little extra for storage. I bought a little propane heater and ordered (May 1999) a Katadyn water filter. I wonder if all of this is silly but think it is better to be ready than sorry. Got the water filter today (May 24, 1999). Cost $259.95 plus tax and I hope we never need it. Also bought a solar powered battery charger.

In January 1999 I bought a new computer. It is a Compaq Presario with an AMD-K6–2 400 Megahertz processor and 128 MB of RAM and a CD-DVD ROM and a 12 GB hard drive and a 17" monitor and lots of other bells and whistles. My old computer had its limitations but I could make it do about anything it was capable of. The new one can do about anything I could ask but I don't know how to make it do it.

Further Developments

Katie is having a really bad time with her hips. If she does anything much like work, she can hardly walk later. I think she is about ready (May 1999) to ask Dr. Larsen for a hip replacement, but that is a major and difficult decision. Update (24 May 1999) Katie will have hip replacement surgery on Friday May 28.

Cody is getting married to Caureen on June 18, 1999 in the Portland Temple and having an open house here on July 10. Steve and Kathy and kids are all coming for that week or two.

May 1999: Steve is quitting his job with the Navy and they are moving to Mt. Pleasant, UT to work with their friends building cabinets for rubber stamps. Kathy and fam then moved to Guatemala to teach for the Rose Foundation for a year but when Kathy found she was pregnant they came home. Steve and Kathy and their six kids—Mari-Xela still to come—moved back to Ashton and I bought the old Alice Rigby home on eight acres six miles south of Ashton. It had been burned quite badly due to a lightning strike but Steve has remodeled it and they are now living in it after living with us for about six months. They got a loan and bought it from me.

November 27, 1999: I write in my journal almost every night but forget about writing in this autobiography. Katie had her operation and is doing fairly well but still has some pain and discomfort and is often discouraged. I am terrific. I've had several successful real estate deals recently. Matt lived with us all summer and worked at Lawson's Island Park Anglers. He loved working there and we loved having him with us. He is going to school now at USU in Logan. Cody and Caureen and Ryan and Wren all came home from college for Thanksgiving but are all going back to school today or tomorrow. Auntie Fay passed away 11/23 and her funeral was 11/26. Velda asked me to give the opening prayer. Not my favorite thing but I guess it was okay.

Connie and Ralph have gone on a mission to Vanuatu. We went

Ralph and Connie Andersen in front of the trailer at the Point, about 2003

to Utah to hear them make their report in sacrament meeting on 10/31/99.

September 2003—Been a long time since I added anything to this biography. Y2K turned out to be a non-event and I am certainly happy about that. Connie and Ralph returned from a very successful mission in Vanuatu. I had kept all their emails and presented them to them in a 3-ring binder as a sort of history of their mission. The Islamic terrorists flew airliners into the World Trade Center and the ensuing economic problems have devastated our country.

The twoth of September was my eightieth birthday. That's old. I finished my "Our Flag" Book for a textbook in the fifth grade and donated fifty copies to the local elementary school. Katie had both hips replaced and gets along quite well. She recently had

Further Developments

Katie and Glade on a bench near the firepit at the Point

cataracts removed from both eyes and again is doing well. A few months ago I began having some urinary problems and on July 25 the family put me in EIRMAC and they removed about two feet of my small intestine which had become gangrenous. The doctors told the family that they thought I had only a 5% chance of surviving. That was six weeks ago and while I am getting stronger all the time, I am still a long way from being as I was before the operation. The doctors told my family that they did not expect me to live through the operation but I did.

Now I'm wondering about having the leaky mitral valve in my heart repaired. Maybe in January. Dr. Hodson said he did not think I should attempt to have the valve repaired and that he thought my kidneys would kill me before my heart did. I am self catheterizing four times a day. Both Katie and I have had cataracts removed from both eyes and are getting along well. It is February 2005 as I write this and my projects are writing a book

Katie and Glade, March 27, 2004

about Ashton's Centennial beginning in 1906. Also transcribing the letters I sent from college and the army to my folks to a Microsoft Word document.[6]

---

6. Glade died on October 10, 2005.

MILITARY HISTORY OF GLADE MARVIN LYON

In the Fall of 1941, I enrolled in Chemical Engineering at the University of Idaho. On December 7th of that year the Japs attacked Pearl Harbor, Hawaii without warning and we were all outraged. I finished that school year and started again the next fall, but decided, along with my friend Jim Barber, to enlist in the U. S. Army. They accepted our applications but told us that since it might be a long war and they might need engineers worse than riflemen, they would let us know when they were ready for us. So I finished that school year and then in June of 1943, I was called to active duty and we entrained for Fort Douglas, Utah where we were outfitted and tested. A few days later we entrained again for North Camp Hood, Texas where we lived in tar-paper-sided barracks. We were in ASTP (Army Specialized Training Program). We spent three months in an infantry basic program: close-order drill, physical fitness, the obstacle course, the infiltration course where we crawled under barbed wire while machine guns were firing live ammunition about three feet above ground level, learning to fire rifles, pistols, machine guns and mortars, and to throw grenades, learning map reading, first aid, hand-to-hand combat, the use of rifle and bayonet, practicing in a simulated German village course, cleaning latrines, scrubbing floors, peeling potatoes, and marching. Central Texas in summer, where temperatures were sometimes said to be 135 degrees, was not too great. If there was shade, we were not allowed to sit in it. Our troops were fighting in North Africa at that time and we were told we were being acclimatized.

We then took a troop train to Bethlehem, Pennsylvania where I was given a third year Electrical Engineering course at Lehigh University. We finished that course in six months and then moved to the Signal Corps School at Fort Monmouth, New Jersey. There I studied telephone circuitry and learned to use and service a "carrier bay," which was a box full of electrical components and circuitry. It was about the size of a casket and weighed 700 pounds but had six handles so it was classified as portable equipment. With it we could take four telephone lines and combine them on one line and connect that to our radios which would send that signal through one or more repeater stations and finally to the destination, where the phone conversations would be sorted out and sent to the correct person. We could substitute as many as four teletype machines for any one voice channel. We had the capability to use facsimile machines (now known as FAX) to transmit maps or other information. It was the very latest in technology for that time. We did field maneuvers in late 1944 in up-state New Jersey, in the rain mostly, testing and learning to use our equipment.

In December of 1944 we took a Liberty Ship across the North Atlantic as the 3186th Signal Service Battalion. It was a two week trip on very rough seas to Liverpool, England. We lived in small rooms at the racetrack in Aintree, England. While we waited for our turn to go to Germany we guarded the docks in Liverpool as they unloaded all sorts of food and other material from the ships. We were on guard twelve hours on and twelve hours off, but one time our relief didn't show up, so we worked our shift and then theirs and then ours again. A Destroyer Escort was tied up at the

Glade ready for cold weather

dock and when they found out that we hadn't been relieved and didn't have any thing to eat, they invited us on board and took us to the officer's mess and handed us a menu. When we found out that we could have our eggs sunny-side-up (our breakfasts at Aintree were powdered eggs, Spam, an English biscuit and awful coffee) we tried to join the Navy. While we were in Liverpool, Sgt. James taught me to love Gilbert and Sullivan Operettas, such as The Mikado and The Pirates of Penzance, as performed by the D'Oyly Carte Opera Company.

In February of 1945 we entrained to Southampton where we boarded a troop ship (climbing a rope ladder with a full pack and a rifle and duffle bag) and crossed the English Channel to France where we took motor launches up the Seine River. We spent the night in tents at Camp Twenty Grand, then marched about five miles to a small town where we took a train. We were in a boxcar marked (in French) forty men or eight horses. There really wasn't room for all of us to lay down, so three of us spent most of the night with our feet hanging out the door, singing "By the Light of the Silvery Moon." The next day at noon, we received C-rations (two small cans, one containing a main dish meal and one containing crackers, powdered coffee, four cigarettes, etc.), just as we stopped at a small town railroad station. I saw a Frenchman sit down and open up his paper sack for lunch, so I jumped off and traded lunches with him. I got a bottle of wine and a loaf of french bread complete with chaff—one of the best meals I've ever eaten. We arrived in Verdun, France that evening and got de-loused. That night we could see the flashes of the big guns as they shelled Germany.

We went to Saarbrucken by truck and set up a communication system linking SHAEF (Supreme Headquarter Allied Expeditionary Forces) with division headquarters at the front. There were five of us on the telephone part and five more on the radios about five miles away on a hilltop. We took over what had been the German Army Headquarters in Saarbrucken. It was an under-

Poster for The Mikado, *D'oyly Carte Opera Company*

ground building with a concrete roof eight foot thick. Calendars on the wall showed that the Germans had left there less than a week earlier. We had electric generators to run our equipment, so we also had electric heaters and hot plates to cook on. We liberated pots and pans and dishes from houses in town. About three days after we got there, we were driving down the street in a jeep when we saw someone duck back into a bombed-out building. He was the first person we had seen in Saarbrucken and assuming he was hostile, we went after him. We didn't find him, but we did find a wine cellar with about fifteen wine casks, (each about eight feet high and twelve feet long). It was about five miles to the nearest watering point and three blocks to the wine cellar. No contest. It is amazing how much better you eat when you take two five gallon cans of wine to trade with when you go to the ration dump. After about two weeks, an Infantry Company moved into Saarbrucken. When we asked why they were there, they told us they had been sent to "hold the town." Made us wonder what we had been doing. We ate with them a time or two and once when we were walking back to our place a machine gun opened up on a truck convoy a few blocks away. Our first instinct was to go stop it, but then we decided that was why the infantry company was there.

Once we went up to our radio installation and went deer hunting. We heard someone coming and saw three men, one of which had a rifle. They were German civilians I guess but we stopped them and took the rifle and a pair of binoculars and a pistol. I took the pistol which was a seven shot revolver with Russian type markings on it. I later traded it for a .25 caliber Mauser automatic.

As the war progressed and the front lines moved forward and the telephone lines were rebuilt we moved from one place to another. Once when we had both our telephones and radios at a little castle on a hilltop, we were buzzed by a small German plane with a bomb under each wing. We had a .50 caliber machine gun on an anti-aircraft mount and some of the guys wanted to try to

Glade with .22 calibre model 37 Winchester

shoot him down but I was the ranking non-com and I said we'd leave him alone if he didn't shoot at us. After a couple of passes he decided we weren't a good enough target and went away.

Once when we had our installation near Wetzlar, I gave a German twelve candy bars and five cartons of cigarettes for a Leica camera (I sold it in Japan for $165). When we left there I had to leave behind a duffle bag full of candy bars and cigarettes. I've often wondered about the person who found that treasure. From there I was attached to the British Second Army near the Belgian border, where four of us ran our equipment in conjunction with a British switchboard. I was able to take a couple of days and go to Brussels. Once two of us were sent to deliver mail to some of the rest of our battalion. We took a small truck and started out but weren't sure we were on the right road when we suddenly came into a town and realized that there were hundreds of German soldiers in the streets. We were really relieved to find out that they were all prisoners of war. Then we were sent to Essen and were there when the Germans surrendered in May of 1945. We went to Weisbaden for about three weeks and then convoyed to Arles in southern France. I found out that my old buddy Jim Barber was in Marseilles and we got together for a couple of parties.

In July we boarded the Matsonia, a troop ship converted from a luxury ocean liner and went through the Panama Canal. We slept on canvas bunks four deep. The heat was terrible and the ventilation the same. We slept on deck sometimes, but the sailors took great delight in hosing us down at dawn. We stopped for one night at Panama City where we spent the night at an Air Force Base (first time on bed sheets for months). Then on across the Pacific. We played a lot of pinochle and a lot of bridge. We stopped at Ulithi Island but didn't get to get off. The atomic bomb was dropped on Japan when we were about half way across the Pacific and we thought we might turn around and go home, but no such luck. We landed in Manila, Philippine Islands on September 2, 1945 which was the day the Japs signed the peace treaty and my

Allied soldiers entering Saarbrucken

Soldier Glade

22nd birthday. We were told that our orders said that we were to have been in the third wave in the invasion of Japan. I might not have made it home if the atomic bomb hadn't been dropped. We set up tents in a swamp, complete with lots of mosquitoes, a mile or so outside Manila. That's where I bought my monkey named Murgatroyd. She was lots of fun but took a lot of care. She liked to ride on my shoulder but she wasn't shoulder broken. After about two weeks we were moved to Lingayen Gulf, a beautiful stretch of sandy beach and palm trees. We had absolutely nothing to do and after a couple of weeks I got so bored I volunteered to be a truck driver.

We went to Japan on an LST (Landing Ship Tank) in October 1945. When we landed on the beach I immediately got my truck stuck in the sand and the rest of the convoy went off and left me. I didn't even know which way to turn. I chose right and I knew that was wrong from the way the people in the tiny village looked at us. So I turned and went the other way and in a few miles I connected up with the convoy. They said they had been driving all the time, so they had been at least as lost as I was. We were barracksed inside Koshien Stadium, half-way between Kobe and Osaka. The devastation was terrible. Our bombers had done their job well. One day I noticed an elderly couple dipping their buckets into our garbage cans and eating it, so I followed them home and then began taking food to them. When I told them I was going home, they gave me their "family sword," a 350 year old Samurai Sword in a plain wooden sheath. A real treasure. I played in a golf tournament in Kobe sponsored by our battalion and won another Samuarai Sword. I was sent home about the first of February on a troop ship. We went to San Francisco and then by train to Fort Lewis, Washington where I was discharged on February 14, 1946 with the rank of Technician Third Grade (a sergeant with five stripes).

I joined the Army to avenge the Japanese sneak attack on Pearl Harbor and to see the world, and did a lot of that. I didn't join

Kobe, Japan, after air raid in 1945

the Navy because I didn't want anything to do with all that water but by the time I got home I had had exactly ninety days at sea. I believe that my time in the service did me more good than any other thing in my life.

Glade Lyon and the National Guard

Shortly after the World War II ended Co. C of the Combat Engineers was organized here in Ashton. I joined and was a Platoon Sergeant. We would meet and drill one evening a week and one weekend a month and two weeks every summer. It was kind of fun and we could use the extra money but about 1952 we were called up for active duty to go to Korea for the "Conflict" there. Captain Cordon made me the Company First Sergeant. Then they called me back for a second medical exam and told me I had a spot on my lung and gave me my discharge. I had my duffel bag packed but had a new son and a new house and a responsibility to my mother in the store so I didn't argue with them.

Mail from Glade to His Parents During His Time at College and in the Army

Thursday 8:00 pm

Sep. 24, 1942
Moscow, Idaho
Dear Folks;
Well, here I am. Tony's not tho. Jim Graves, a fellow I met on the train and I are in a three man room and waiting for Tony to take the other 1/3. Bud and Elden are living up town. All my luggage got here but it's not unpacked yet. I'm going to take the final tomorrow at 8:00 A.M. Love, Glade
Glade Lyon—Box 70—Lindley Hall—Moscow, Ida.

Saturday afternoon

Oct. 27, 1942
Lindley Hall

Moscow, Idaho

Well, here I am listening to the football game. Last week and this Tony has been running a football pool. He picks two games and then whoever picks the most winners wins the pot. Jim, I and another fellow tied for it last week. So I made 50¢. And this week maybe I'll do it again.

I lost my pen (that old $1.00 one) sometime this week or else someone stole it, so I'm writing this with my new $5.00 Sheaffer I bought today. It just matches that Sheaffer pencil I have. Is that okay?

I got the meal ticket when we first got here. We didn't get any meals for a day and a half and I knew we'd be wanting some milk shakes too.

Ted sent me a money order the other day so I've got that $13. And thanks for the money. I don't need it much tho. Not too much anyhow.

Here it is Monday morning already. I interrupted to go to supper, then I had a date. Sunday morn we played golf and Sunday afternoon went to a darn good show. Then I had Physics to do all nite.

Remember, I bought the new pen Saturday? Well, yesterday Jim was going through a bunch of papers and found the old one—so now I have two.

We still don't know much about the reserves. The term of enlistment is the duration + six months. As soon as we're out of school we're supposedly given 13 weeks of basic training, then 13 weeks of Officers Candidate school and (if we're still in the running) finally to Officers Training School. They tell us we'll be permitted to stay in school as long as possible but don't give anything definite on it. The sophomore class president is in the reserves (ERC) and he seems to think he'll be able to stay in school that way longer than any other way. But we can be called anytime. I guess I'll try to get in. What do you think?

I got my glasses and I've been wearing them some but I'm not

Tuesday nite 117

supposed to wear them for close work and so it's sort of bad. And if I wear them too long, I get sort of a headache.

I got some application blanks for N.Y.A. work because that's about the only place I can get work in the periods I have free. But I found out that I can't get the work unless I am absolutely unable to get through without it. Well, it's 1:00 o'clock and I've gotta go to chemistry.

4:30—Just talking to Bill Kerr. Says he's figuring on joining the ERC because after next July there will be no educational deferments and he's pretty sure he can stay out longer if he joins the ERC.

Just called the Dean of Men and they say they would like the ERC's to attend the summer term but it will not be insisted upon.

Had a Calculus quiz several days ago on which I got 92, also a chem. Quiz: 96 and a Physics quiz that I got a 48 on but the class average was about 35 and they grade on the curve so that's about a "B." But it seems like I'm always behind.

Seems I had something more to say but can't think. Thanks to Connie for her swell letter a while back and love to all. Glade

Glade Lyon—Box 70—Lindley Hall—Moscow, Idaho

Tuesday nite

Box 70 Lindley Hall
Moscow, Idaho
Dear Folks,

Sitting here listening to the radio and trying to write but I'm not doing so well at the writing. Don't know what to say.

Hope Connie is better. We've been having some awful weather, but I haven't caught cold.

I'm having quite a bit of trouble with my studies. The grades aren't so high. Just seems I don't have time to study everything that I need to. Had a chem quiz today that I sure didn't do very good on.

Garold Troth and Floyd Griffel were here the other night. Sure was a surprise. They'd been to Spokane and brought Janeal down to see Elden.

I told you Mildred was probably going to California didn't I? So I'll be a widower except for Artis. I think you're wrong about Tonna and Bob. It will last I'm quite sure. They're pretty much in love.

I'm sorry Peggy is homesick. I wrote to her a few days ago and today I got it back with a "No Such an Address" written on it. So I changed it from So. State to So. Temple and I'm sending it back.

Tried to get into the Army Air Force Reserves in the Armament division of the ground crew, but I have to have completed two years of engineering (three to get in engineering). And I found out that there are no reserves for the ground crew. So—I'll just wait to see if I can't get thru the year. If I can I think I'll enlist in the Armament. If not, I have my papers about ready to enlist in the E.R.C.'S unassigned.

Don't worry about the cookies, they're not worth the trouble I guess. And don't pay much attention to the Xmas presents. Haven't much choice except it shouldn't be clothes cause I can't wear them after I'm in the service. A billfold or a pair of ping pong paddles maybe—doesn't matter so long as it isn't very much. Signing off with love, Glade

Box 70—Lindley Hall—Moscow, Idaho

Sunday morning

12/6/1942
Moscow, Idaho
Dear Folks-

I was sure glad to get your letter. It was such a good one too. I guess I must be getting just a little homesick. Did I thank you for the box you sent? I can't remember for sure. It sure was good anyway.

I'm sorry to hear about Leon. It's sure too bad.

We have a little snow and more coming down now. The roads are awfully slick. There's a hill the fellows slide down that's about 2 blocks long. Some slippery slide huh? Three guys in the infirmary though.

Mildred and I went shopping yesterday and I bought a few things but I have an awful time knowing what to get. I don't think too much of Connie's birthday present but I couldn't find anything I thought she'd like. Tell Velda she'll have to wait for Xmas on account of her birthday and Christmas presents are all rolled into one. Haven't seen any of the items you mentioned for Velda. I got something for Grandma and Grandpa too.

Eides were figuring pretty definitely on going to California once but the work at Bayview lasted longer than was planned and I haven't heard much about the moving lately.

Good for Aunt Daisy!!!

I've written to Artis a few times but not much. I have three dates with her at Xmas but now that gas rationing has arrived I guess I'd better call at least one off. I thought maybe I could take the car one night to see her and Hemming could get his one night. How do you like gas rationing, by the way?

Thanks for the money. I'll get home on it O.K. That is if I have a way. Everybody is wondering how to get there. How? Jim and I bought each other a tie for Xmas. Wait'll you see mine. Love, Glade

Telegram

Feb. 1, 1943
Spokane, Was.
J T Lyon
Happy birthday Dad. I'm on vacation in Spokane. Have probable C average and so can stay in school until June. Will write soon. Love, Glade

Saturday morning

February 22, 1943
Moscow, Idaho
Dear Folks,

Well, I still don't know anything about the army. They called a bunch of E.R.C. at W.S.C. the other day but we haven't heard anything yet.

I'm taking a lot of hours all right but I think I can do it. Bill Kerr (another chem. engineer) and I are both taking exactly the same course. He's a little smarter than I am but I guess I'll get through.

Jim and I moved into room 210 after Tony left and I got another roommate. He's one of these kids who haven't finished high school yet. War-babies we call them. I don't like him too well. Oh, we get along but he's sort of a funny kid.

About getting married, I agree with what you said. I've thought that all the time but I wanted to know what you thought. I don't think her folks especially want it but if Mildred wanted to they wouldn't say anything. And Mildred wants to, so -. But we will wait until after the war.

All of my morning classes except P.E. and War-Chem-Physics. I have 2 physics labs and two chem. labs each week and 1 survey lab. The surveying is fun because we get to work outside. They're giving us quite a workout in P.E. We get some pretty stiff calisthenics. I was kinda sore and stiff the fist week but it's not bad now. I've lost a little weight in P.E. but I think it'll come back soon. Mildred and I went to a semiformal dance Friday and had a lot of fun. And I think we're going on a hike tomorrow afternoon.

It's spring up here. The snow is almost all gone. And people are roller skating and bicycling and getting out golf clubs and tennis rackets. And the sun is warm on your back when you take off your shirt. Well, I've gotta study darn it. Write soon. Love, Glade

Mrs. Eide made me a big angel food cake for Valentine's.

Thanks lots for the cookies and candy and valentine , they were awfully nice.

Sorry I didn't get this letter off but I didn't have a stamp.

Glade Lyon—Lindley Hall- Moscow, Idaho

Mar. 6, 1943

Moscow, Idaho

Dear Folks,

Sorry I've been so slow writing again but I've been having some quizzes and it seems like I have to study every time I sit down at the desk.

I've been over to the chem. lab. all morning trying to get a little ahead, but I didn't accomplish very much. School is sort of tough. Seems like I study quite a bit but my grades aren't any too high.

I hope Velda is O.K.

Mr. Eide has been working at Mountain Home but he's not feeling very good so he came home the other day. I don't know just how long he'll stay though.

About 75 (I think it was) of the E.R.C.'s got called for March 18 the other day but my name wasn't on the list. There are rumors floating around that we will be gmsen our basic training during the summer. But nobody seems to know. We also hear we are going to have a few hundred soldiers on the campus to study engineering. We're wondering now where they'll put them.

That snow sure looks awful. It's spring up here. I haven't remembered to look for a knife when I've been in town yet but I will soon. Clothes are holding our O.K. I guess. I would like a sport coat but it costs too much money. I don't need anything else much I guess. I'd like a pair of shoes and a lot of other stuff but I can't afford it and I'm afraid I couldn't wear it when I get out of the army.

How is rationing affecting you? We're only getting ½ as much butter as usual and don't seem to be getting fed very well but I guess we'll live.

My bank balance is pretty low but I'll get by.

I've got a new roommate. Ken Oliver, the war baby pledged and so Colin Stebbins the kid that was rooming with Bon Bernhart. He's sure a nut and we got along find. Mildred and I bicycled to Pullman last Saturday. Had quite a bit of fun. We're going to a fireside at the Teke house tonite.

I'm sending you some pictures I took. They've got names and dates on the back. I've also some negatives I haven't had prints made of and I'll send them soon. Love, Glade

Oh yes, If I get to come home in June I'm going to bring Mildred. Or did I tell you?

Take good care of the pictures.

Glade Lyon—Lindley Hall—Moscow Idaho

Mar. 18, 1943

Moscow, Idaho
Dear Folks,
Got my call today. Am to be in Fort Douglas June 17. Will leave here for Ashton, May 30. That would get me there 31st. Will have to be here to report on the 15th I think. Want to leave Ashton 10th. Thus will get out of "Pocy" the 11th and get here the 12th and spend 13 and 14 with Mildred. Write soon. Love, Glade

Thursday nite

March 21, 1943
Moscow, Idaho
Dear Folks,
Gosh it sure seems good to hear from you. Sseems like I haven't had a letter for weeks and weeks.

We've been having pretty fair weather here although it has

Thursday nite

been just a little too cool for comfort. A week ago yesterday I had a surveying lab and I was out about 4 hours in the cold. So I've had a heck of a cold since. It's quite a bit better now tho. Just about gone.

Those E.R.C.s who left school at the semester are to go the 27th and they have to leave from here. Got a letter from Jim today—he says he'll get here the 25th. In a way I'd like to be going along.

They've sure been keeping us busy lately. We had a Physics Quiz Monday, a War-Physics-Chem Quiz the Friday before that, a Surveying Quiz Tuesday, and a Calculus and Military Quiz today. So I haven't been fooling around much. Nothing much important tomorrow tho so a bunch of us went to the show tonight.

Did you get the Argonauts?

There's a fireside tomorrow nite Mildred and I are going to. We went on a "Victory Ball" last Friday and the Engineer's Ball Saturday. Had lot of fun at the Engineer's Ball.

The E.R.C.s called for the 18th were all the E.R.C.s except sophs, juniors, or seniors taking engineering, medicine, dentistry, etc.

I've been thinking of trying to get in the Meteorology Division of the Army but I'm not too sure if I want it. What do you think? And I'm not sure if I can get in if I want to. I'm going to find out tomorrow.

Thanks for the money. I wish you'd send me a new check book. Mine's all worn out. I sure am having a hard time to keep any money this year. Last year I saved enough to buy some shoes and a sport coat and such but this year I can't save any. I'm always broke just before you put the $25 in. I guess it's because board is higher—I don't know.

I don't know anything about what I'll do this summer. Write soon. Love, Glade

If Mom hasn't anything else to do she could bake some cookies and send them up. But don't worry about it.

If I do get to come home in the summer tho, I'd just as soon stay there. Probably won't get to be around long.

Glade Lyon—Lindley Hall—Moscow, Idaho

April 17, 1943

Moscow, ID
Dear Folks,
Well, they did it again. The army is moving into Lindley and we have to be out by Monday, midnite. We've been to town looking for apartments and may move back where I lived last spring or we may move to the Idaho Club. Don't know yet. I'll write a letter as soon as I can but this well keep me busy awhile and too I have several quizzes next week so I probably won't write until Wednesday. Love, Glade
Glade Lyon—Lindley Hsall—Moscow, ID

May 12, 1943

Idaho Club
Moscow, Idaho
Dear Folks;
I'll see if I can write you a little letter before dinner. Thanks a million for the cookies. They tasted awfully good but they didn't last long. All three of my roommates said to tell you thanks. Our four man room is coming along fine so far.

I'm supposed to be hashing this week but we have to go to military at 7 A.M. all this week to drill for the final inspection Friday so I couldn't work in the morning and I was afraid I'd better use all my time to study for my finals so I hired a fellow to do it for me.

I have two finals Wed. May 26 and two May 27. Then my last one is Sat. the 29th. The War-Phys-Chem. final isn't scheduled yet but I imagine it will be earlier than any of them. It if it is, I'll be starting for home either Monday or Tuesday—depends on—.

I still don't know what the ERC is going to say. But I'm pretty

Aug. 9, 1943

sure I'll be taking my 13 weeks of basic training this summer. What am I going to do with all my stuff? I've been sort of thinking of leaving my radio and typewriter with Mildred. She hasn't got a radio and she's been taking typing with and needs something to practice on (she had a typewriter for quite a while). What do you think? I haven't even asked her if she wants them yet but I think she would like to have them. Thought I'd see what you thought before I said anything.

We went up to Tekos to the Junior Prom Friday and had a lot of fun. I told you we were going didn't I? We went to a little party afterward and had a fine time. Mildred's mother said everyone in the looking-on crowd was talking about us.

The dinner bell just rang so I'll close.

Glade Lyon—Idaho Club—Moscow, Idaho

Aug. 9, 1943

North Camp Hood, Texas
Dear Folks,
Welll, it's 11 p.m. I'm in Waco again and I haven't a thing to do. I'm so darn tired I can hardly stand it but the train doesn't leave until 112:15.

Yesterday morning I went on sick call to get some glasses. I started out at about 7 A.M. and didn't get back until 5 P.M., and all I had done was sit around all day. When they got started it took about 15 minutes to do everything so I was thoroughly disgusted with the medical dept.

Then at 7:30 last night we started on a 10 mile hike. It was our longest so far. wWe got back at 10:30 and then we had to prepare for the inspection this morning. So I didn't get to bed until 12:30—I got up at 4:00 and started getting more ready for the inspection. The inspection was rough but a lot from our barracks passed it so we all headed for Waco. We also got paid Friday so we had lots of money. I got $49.25 and it's gone already.

It sure goes fast. I can easily see why guys send home for money. Seems like the business people try to take the enlisted men for all they've got. I bought a shirt for $3.50, and I paid $5.50 to have my picture taken for you and Mildred. It'll probably be about a month before you get it though. Then the train ticket was 75¢ and we had to eat two meals and food is sky high. And we have to have something to drink every 10 minutes or so because we sweat so much and it's so hot. All in all I've spent between $15 and $20 today. And it doesn't seem like I've wasted hardly any at all. No more than the others I know. I bought a belt buckle for $1.00 and shoe and leggin laces and all sorts of things.

Say, will you send me some undershirts? I've got some home someplace I think. We have to wear a clean one all the time and I've only got three so it is sort of hard for me to do sometimes. And send me that big thick book of mine too will you. It's got a heavy gray paper cover on it and it's got ESHBACH printed twice on the cover. I think. I can't remember right where it is though. Be sure and pack it well. I want to keep it in good shape. I don't know whether you've heard me speak of Joy Rogers or not. She's one of Mildred's friends. She's getting married tonight to a sailor. Mildred is the bridesmaid and she certainly is excited she's been telling me all about it for the last two weeks. And she seems to wish it were us. I do to. It would be nice we think.

It's getting about time to start for the station so I'll close for now and finish this sometime tomorrow.

Hello folks,

How's everything? Had a pretty good sleep last night—got up just in time for dinner. Then Jim and I showered and washed our fatigues and went to the show. Just got back.

While I think of it, I wanted to know if Dad ever got those razor blades I put in the suitcase. If he wants anymore I can buy them and send them up. The army has lots of them.

Jim says if I ever get sick or anything he'll let you know so don't worry any about me until you find out I'm not O.K.

August 16, 1943

You ask what I want for my birthday. Well, I'm very certain I don't know. I've got about everything I need and what I don't have I can get here easier than you can get it and send it to me.

I may buy a pair of shoes if I decide I have enough money. They've got some at the PX for $7.50. But I'm about broke. I bought a book of theater tickets and some razor blades today and I've got just $30.04 left out of my pay. I was figuring on paying you back the money I owe you but I don't think I can make it this time and if it goes this fast every time I'm going to have to be at least a colonel before I have enough money to pay it. And that's quite a way to go. I guess I can send you some next payday though. Jim wants to go to Austin next week end but I'm afraid I'm too near broke and Jim doesn't have as much as I have so I don't know what he's figuring on spending.

The fellows say next week is going to be awfully tough. I haven't seen the schedule yet but I hear we're going on some night maneuvers but I'm not at all sure. We'll probably work all day and hike all night or something.

Mildred said she and her mother were bottling raspberries, too. You guys better all bottle lots of stuff because the man in the Reader's Digest says we're going to have a food shortage.

Well, this is a pretty long letter for me. I guess I'd better close and go to chow. I'll write again soon as I get a chance. Love, Glade

Pvt. Glade M. Lyon—Co. A 132 ASTB—North Cap Hood, Texas

August 16, 1943

Bar 4 Co. A
143 ASTB 6th Reg.
Dear Folks,

Hello how's everybody? There are big things doing down here. We've moved. I'm now in the 143rd Battalion. We'd heard a lot of rumors about it and had a pretty good idea we were moving but didn't know for sure until yesterday. Over here we have a little better deal I believe. We have company mess hall instead of battalion mess. That should make better meals and less waiting in line. We've only had one meal here but it was better than we've been getting. Also, all our officers and non-coms are infantrymen, where most of them were tank destroyers at the 132nd. My address is now:

Pvt. Glade M. Lyon 19119746
Bar. 4, Co. A, 143 A.S.T.B.
6 Regiment
North Camp Hood, Texas

It'll probably be changed slightly soon though. I'll give you the new version as soon as I find out what it is.

I didn't have any time to write last week. They keep us pretty busy all the time. We went on an eight mile hike Tuesday night and a ten miler Friday morning. We've been having a lot of stuff on extended order drill too, and how to hit the dirt and take cover or camouflage ourselves. Also how to use a compass. One night we had to cover a one mile course after dark through trees and stuff and had to come out at the right place. We didn't have any trouble though. But we didn't get back to the barracks until after one ayem so we didn't get much sleep.

I cut this letter short a while ago and had chow and went to the show. It's about 10:15 now. Had a pretty good meal again tonight. We seem to have a very good setup here. Our cadre seem pretty good and they talk as though they were going to be easier on us than our others were. I think we'll like it better all around. And best of all we've got only seven more weeks of training.

Guess Dad is O.K. now. Did he catch a lot of fish?

Today is the 14th again. So I've been engaged a whole two months. Fun huh? It's been just 18 months since Mildred and I had our first date. You don't think we should be married when I finish here? She does. She has never told me much about her folks opinion though except that they think she should finish high school. She could finish high school after we were married though.

I can see why you think we should wait and I agree with you in part but I know that we both love each other and I myself am afraid that we may not have another chance to be together. I want to have as much happiness with her as I can. My lifetime may not be very long.

How's the weather up there? It's been hot again lately here. There are nut and fruit trees around here but nothing is ripe yet. The apricots should be ripe in about two weeks though.

Well folks, it's getting pretty late so I'd better close. Write soon. Love, Glade

Had my picture taken and here's the proof I didn't like. Thot you'd like to see it.

Pvt. Glade M. Lyon—Bar. 4, Co. A. North Camp Hood Texas—Co. A—143 A.S.T.B.

North Camp Hood, Texas

Sunday night
Aug. 23, 1943
Dear folks,

It's after 10:00 and lights are out so I'll just write enough to let you know I'm still alive and then I'll hit my bunk.

Had a pretty tough inspection yesterday but I passed so I got a pass. This new outfit we're in gives out weekend passes so Jim and Potvin and I were thinking of going someplace but we finally didn't do much. Just wandered around camp and went into Gatesville for a few hours.

Did I tell you I was a squad leader? Well, I am. I guess it'll be a permanent job unless I mess something up. I don't like it much though. I've too much responsibility and too little authority. I'm sort of an acting corporal (so they said) but the men won't take orders from me very good because I'm actually only a private. But I'm the one that gets cussed when things go wrong.

We had a night problem Tuesday night. Short march to an area to dig slit trenches and an actual gas attack on the way (tear gas). Also one Thursday night. Had to infiltrate through enemy lines. Crawling on our bellies and such stuff. I hear we're going on a 10 mile march tomorrow with full field pack but I don't know for sure.

Had a good dinner today. Chicken, dressing, candied sweet potatoes, ice cream. First such meal I've seen.

Guess I'd better go to bed Love, Glade

Got the book and undershirts. Thanx a lot. Also for candy.

Pvt. Glade M. Lyon—Co. A. 143 A.S.T.B.—North Camp Hood, Texas

Aug. 30 1943

No. Camp Hood, Texas
Dear Folks,
Thot you might like this (Postcard titled "Hell in Texas"). It's a perfect description of what I've seen of Texas.

Pvt. Glade M. Lyon—Co. A—143 ASTP—No. Camp Hood , Texas

Sunday night

August 31, 1943
North Camp Hood, Texas
Dear Folks,
I really should be in bed but I put off writing all day so I guess I'd better do it now. We had a pretty hard week last week. Thursday we had a 10 mile march in the morning, in the afternoon we had classes as usual and at night we had a motor march (marched six miles and rode three). Friday morning we dug fox holes and had class and in the afternoon we cleaned up for inspection. Saturday morning we had inspection and it went off pretty smooth.

I hear we take some tests tomorrow but I don't know for sure. I also hear that part of us may be shipped out after out tenth week of training so I may not be here much longer. At any rate we only have 5 weeks of training left out of the original 13. We also start firing the machine gun next week. Fun huh?

I'm sending you some stuff soon as I get to the postoffice. I've got it all wrapped and addressed but haven't any stamps. Say folks, about that money I owe you—I don't suppose I'm ever going to get it paid back while I'm a private in the army. Is it O.K. with you if I subscribe to a full bond every month because I know I can't save any other way? Let me know. Maybe I can pay it back when I get to be a civilian again. Write Soon. Love, Glade

Use address on front.

Pvt. Glade Lyon—Bar 4, Co A.—143 A.S.T.B.—North Camp Hood, Texas

Pvt. Glade M. Lyon

Co. A 143 ASTB
North Camp Hood, Texas
Dear Folks,

I got your package and opened it yesterday but I didn't get to write last night. Anyway thanks a million. I like the writing folder and the stationery very much. The socks I don't need now but they'll come in handy later. Thanks again and most of all for the money—it seems like that's one thing I don't ever have enough of. Maybe if you send me enough as gifts I can sometime pay back that that I owe you. My birthday isn't until tomorrow but I've already got your package and one from Grandma and Grandpa. Grandma and Grandma sent me a check for $7.50 and a big box which I haven't opened yet but Grandpa said he thought contained a cake. Which reminds me that I haven't eaten any of the cookies—? are they cookies? I haven't looked—you sent. But thanks a lot for them. I wanted to wait until there weren't too may fellows around because everyone wants a share and it'll only go so far. Any food will be well taken care of.

We were on the machine gun range all day yesterday. Browning Light Machine Gun HBM 1918 A 4 ground (whatever that is) is what we were shooting. It sure is fun—just squeeze back on the trigger and hold it there and away they go. I made a score of 215 out of a possible 256. That makes me a first class gunner. Best is expert (above 217) last is second class gunner (180 to 200). Anything less than 180 isn't qualifying.

Just broke this off and went over to the PX but I'm back now as you can plainly see. I opened the cookies and ate about six—but there were a few too many men present so there are only about two left. They were sure good.

Mildred said she had sent for a present for me but that it didn't come in time so it would be a little later. I'm sure I don't know what it could be.

About the picture—I intended to go into Waco last week end and get it but I changed my mind so I wrote and asked them to be sent to me here and then I'll send it. I sent you a card table cover and eight packages of razor blades. Did you get it O.K.?

Night before last we took an ASTP test. Is think I did pretty fair but I don't know for sure. I'm qualified to go into the advanced engineering course if I make out OK in the next three tests. They're pretty tough tests tough so I may not make it. If not I go into the basic course. I'm positive that I'll make that. One company has taken all their tests and had their interviews and there was only one man who is not going back to school.

Well, it's time for lights out so goodnight. Thanks again for everything.

Love to all, Glade

Pvt. Glade M. Lyon—Co. A 143 ASTB—North Camp Hood Texas

Pvt. Glade M. Lyon

Co. A 143 ASTB
North Camp Hood, Texas
Dear Folks,

I'm on guard tonight so I've got a little time before I start walking my post. I'm on from 13:30 until. We're really on the alert tonight because 4 German prisoners escaped last night. We always walk guard with fixed bayonets and five rounds in the magazine but this seems to gives us a real reason for it. It's been raining today. We went to the mortar range this afternoon to see a demonstration and to fire the mortar but it rained so hard they called it off and we came back in.

Sunday we go on the battle conditioning course and come back Tuesday. And the next Sunday we go on a bivouac and get back Wednesday. That's the end of our basic and then it won't be long (oh happy day) until I'll be in school. Jim Graves is in ASTP too you know. He's finished his basic now and is going to school at the University of California in Berkeley. I sure hope I get to go back to Idaho. I want to be as close to that gal of mine as I can while I have the chance. Is told her in a letter the other day that if I get a furlough at Christmas (and I heard that we do), that she is to meet me at Ashton. That's if I don't go to school at Idaho—if I do she can come right along with me. I haven't heard from her yet, but I might as well talk you both into it at the same time. This is Friday noon. I was called out back there a couple of lines. Had a very uneventful walk on guard. Saw and challenged only two persons all night.

This morning we marched about 5 miles out to the mortar range and did the firing that was to come yesterday. Each two fellows got to fire one shell between them so didn't do much but it was interesting. We got to ride most of the way back.

Another fellow and I are going over to the hospital this afternoon and get the G.I. glasses we ordered a long time ago.

I'm sending a little pamphlet on Lutheran beliefs I thought Mother might like to read. I picked it up in Austin.

It's time for me to go now so I'll close. Love, Glade

P.S. Tell my grandparents I'll write to them as soon as I get time but it may not be for awhile.

Pvt. Glade M. Lyon—Co. A 143 ASTB—North Camp Hood, Texas

Western Union

Oct. 5, 1943
Bethlehem. Penn.
J. T. Lyon
Arrived today like it very well my address Co. G First Platoon 3309 Service Unit Lehigh University. Glade

Saturday night

Sep. 20, 1943
North Camp Hood, Tex.
Dear Folks;
Just time for a short note. We start on the B.C. course tomorrow and don't get back until Wed. so don't expect to hear from me for a couple of days. I bought myself a pair of shoes today. Cost me $6.50. Guess they're O.K. Feel just a little tight but not bad. Rumor says we may ship as soon as we're back. Got work to do so I'll close. Love, Glade

Pvt. Glade M. Lyon—Co. A 143 A.S.T.B.—North Camp Hood, Tex.

Date illegible 1943

Bethlehem, Pa.
Dear Folks,

Please send me my Calculus book, my gym shoes, shorts, sweat shirt and all that gym equipment (it's all together). Also send my engineering scales (maybe rulers to you)(they're triangular like this. Love, Glade

Pfc. Glade Lyon—Co. C 3309 A.S.T.P.—Bethlehem, Pa.

Sept. 28, 1943

No. Camp Hood. TX

Dearest Mom;

Im wishing you a very happy birthday, but I'm having a hard time letting you know about it. I should have written several days ago I guess, but I'd sory of temporarily forgotten your birthday. We were on the rifle range all day today. Got up at 4:30 and didn't get in until 8:00. I put on my suntans and was just going to go call you on the phone when I got orders to report to the mess hall. It was 9:30 when I left there. I went over and placed my call but the operator said it wouldn't go through for several hours so I canceled it. Then I went to the telegraph office but I found out I couldn't send any greetings of any sort. So, I'm doing the next best. Anyway, I hope you've had a happy birthday. I'd sure like to be with you for a while.

It's a lot cooler today. We were in the pits all morning and on the range in the afternoon. In practice firing I was one point short of making sharpshooter. (That's between average and excellent). I hope I can make it when we fire for record but I doubt it.

This is a short letter but I only got 5 ½ hours of sleep last nite and it's about 11:00 now so I'll close and write more soon. Purty stayshunary ain't it? (written on Tank destroyer stationery.) All my love, Glade

Pvt. Glade M. Lyon—Co. A 132 A.S.T.B.—No. Camp Hood, Texas

Tuesday morning

Oct. 21, 1943
Lehigh U.
Bethlehem, Pa.
Dear Folks,

I'm in a class but it's pretty boring so I'll write you a note. I hope you're not expecting many letters from me because we're kept so busy I just don't have time to write.

We had quite a time in New York City. It's really a service man's town. They just about gave us the place it seemed. We stayed at the Y.M.C.A. They took my pictures free and offered to make free recordings of our voices and gave us a free tour of the city. The tour was pretty good. We went down to Battery Park & Wall Street. Saw the spot where Washington made his inaugural speech.

Wednesday morning

Hi -

Here I am again 24 hours later in the same class. I hope I get this finished today. To go on with what we did in N.Y.C. We saw the Stage Door Canteen, Radio City, Sardi's, Jack Dempsey's restaurant, the Statue of Liberty from the top of the Empire State Building, Times Square, Grand Central Station, Penn Station, City Hall, Waldorf-Astoria and Biltmore Hotels and a lot more. We rode on a subway several times but it wasn't very exciting.

We met two English sailors when we were leaving the "Y" to go on the tour. We were with them for several hours and had some interesting talks with them.

We also got some of the new shoulder insignia for A.S.T.P. We've got the only ones on the campus here now. They're sort of pretty.

Just before I left North Camp, someone stole a pair of O.D. pants from me. I signed the paper to have the money for another pair taken out of my pay but I didn't get the pants and now

Wednesday morning

I'm having a lot of trouble trying to get them here. I think I'll borrow some money and buy a pair at a retail store here. Then I'll probably have to borrow some from you to pay them back. I don't know what to do. I need the pants but I'm practically flat broke after that trip to N.Y.C.

Yes, I got the sewing kit and it's nice but I haven't sent a thank you note. I don't even know her address. I just don't have time to write. And I'm afraid I should have written Grandma & Grandpa long ago. I just don't have time.

As far as my Xmas present is concerned there's only one thing I can think of that I want now and that's a uniform.

Wednesday evening

I bought a new cap (with blue braid—that stands for infantry—and a little pair of crossed rifles on it). It's really pretty. But now I need a uniform to match it. It's darker than G.I. issue olive drabs. The kind officers wear. The only trouble is it costs (the uniform) more than it's worth I'm afraid.

I've been using Jim's pen here. Mine ran out of ink.

Is guess I'll just buy a pair of ordinary kind O.D. pants. Or something, I dunno.

I got the Herald today. Haven't had time to read it though. I thought I'd maybe get the other stuff today but I didn't. Tomorrow probably.

They're trying to teach me how to swim but they're not making much progress. I had my first lesson for two hours this afternoon. I was just about scared to death. They put me and one other fellow in a class all by our selves and he was doing quite a lot better than I was so you can see I was quite low on the list of swimmers. I don't know whether I'll ever make the grade or not. For goodness sake, make sure that Connie learns now to swim and skate and ski and everything elso. She'll certainly be glad when she gets older.

Speaking of my kid Sis, how old is she? I can't even remember for sure. And what does she want for Xmas? I'm sure I haven't any ideas.

Just got back from going to chow and then to town for a few minutes. I priced a pair of OD pants. $11.97 and $18.00 so I guess I won't be buying any of them. I've got to start studying now. We have several quizzes coming up this week end and the first of next week.

Oh yes, I'm taking Calculus, Mechanics, Shop Lab., Electrical engineering, Electrical Measurements Lab. Physical Training, Military Theory and Drill and Rifle Practice.

I'd better quit now. Love, Glade

Pfc. Glade M. Lyon—Co. C 3309 ASTU—Lehigh U.—Bethlehem, Pa.

Pfc. Glade Lyon

Co C 3309 SU
Bethlehem, Pa.
Dear Folks,
I've got a few extra minutes so guess I'll answer your last letter.

I've still got my cold but it's not as bad as it was. My nose runs all the time but other than that I'm OK.

My room is right across the hall from Jim's, but I'm in his room most of the time. We do all our studying together. Ed Blair is a fellow from Nevada who as been with us ever since we were at Fort Douglas. He's a nice kid.

I don't think Mildred minds if I go with my other girls if I don't do too much of it. We decided it'd be OK. She's been going out once in a while. As long as it's not too often I guess it's OK What do you think?

I've done about all my Xmas shopping. I picked out a locket that I guess I'll send to Mildred. I thought I might have my picture taken but I didn't get it done yet. Maybe I'll do it after Xmas sometime and send Grandma one then.

The weather is quite cold here most of the time and we get a little rain, but we haven't had any snow at all.

I heard from Gene a couple of times. He seems to like it OK.

We just got through a tough Calculus quiz a little while ago. It was not so had but it was so long I only got a little over half finished. I've got a 60 average so hope I didn't do too badly. All my other grades are OK. I've a 90 average in Mechanics and a 90 in Electricity (not counting the last quiz, which we haven't got back yet). And those are the most important subjects so I'm not doing too bad.

Jim and Margy and I took some kodak pictures a while back. I'll send a couple of them as soon as we have some made.

Guess I'll do just about the same thing this week end as usual. See a couple of shows or something.

Oh say, what's the chance of getting some great big Idaho potatoes out in this part of the country? Could you get me some extra big no. 1s. from Oliver or somebody and send them without it costing too much. There are some of the Pennsylvania people I've met I'd like to give some to, for their Xmas dinners. Jim got a few pretty nice ones and everybody's eyes popped our when they saw them. We saw some Idaho potatoes on sale in New York for 20 cents each. Good price huh?

I've a class soon so I'll close.

Love, Glade

Pfc. Glade Lyon—Co C 3309 SU—Bethlehem Pa.

Saturday afternoon

Jan. 17, 1944
Bethlehem, Pa.
Dear Folks,

I'm sorry I don't write to you more often. I know I should but I dislike writing letters so, and I really don't have much time.

I guess I didn't tell you much about my furlough did I? I could have gone to Washington but I wanted to stop off in Phily too and then since the weather ws bad I didn't think I'd get to do much sight-seeing in Washington. Anyway so I'd just stay in Phily. I had the money to buy a ticket but I didn't think there was any use to spend it that way. Hitch-hiking is very easy for fellows in the service. Both to and from Phily I made better time than the train. I had a pretty fair time. I got back here Thursday and stayed over at the house Jim's wife stays at until Sunday. Had quite a lot of fun and a real nice rest.

I really don't know how my test came out. We've never heard but they must have been O.K. because I'm still here. Four fellows from my section flunked out. There are only 25 of us left.

I got your telegrams. In fact, I got two copies of the first one. I don't know why tho. You didn't need to send the one about the Christmas package. I had the packages a couple of days before I got the telegram.

We've been having a real cold spell with about 2 inches of snow on the ground for the last two weeks but it warmed p a little yesterday, and we got about ½ inch of snow last night. It's been thawing all day today though.

I'm going to have to do an awful lot of studying this term I'm afraid. Last term I'd had all the subjects so I got by comparatively easily, but this term its all new material so I'll have to get on the ball. It's interesting though and I'm learning a little so I don't mind. We have two electricity courses (Alternating Current Circuits, and Direct Current Machinery) and they're both interesting. I haven't had quite as much background in electricity as I need to understand all the material but I get most of it fairly well. We had a test in A. C. Saturday. It was very simple but I made a couple of errors in copying the problems so I didn't get either of the two problems correct. They won't count off too much tho, I hope.

I was section marcher last week. That's the guy that marches the section to class and stuff like that. We take turns. But it's a thankless job and I'm glad it's over.

The Boyd Miner Family sent me some real nice handkerchiefs and a tie for Xmas.

Saturday afternoon

Well, guess I'd better close. I've got some more letters to write and some studying to do. Love, Glade

P.S. Mildred's birthday (No. 18 is the 23rd of this month. I send her an identification bracelet.

Pfc. Glade Lyon—Co. C. 3309 A.S.T.U.—Bethlehem, Pa.

Saturday afternoon

????????? 1944
Bethlehem, Pa.
Dear Folks,

My furlough's just about over. We have to be back at 9 tomorrow morning. So guess I'd better write a note to you.

I haven't done much on this furlough. I was in Philadelphia for 3 days and had a pretty good time there. I intended to go to Washington but it rained so all the time that I decided it wasn't worth while.

I say two good stage shows in Phily and the rest of the time I just stayed around the U.S.O.s. There were about five or six real nice U.S.O.s and the Stage Door Canteen there is better than the one in New York I think. I was at the Stage Door Canteen almost all evening Wednesday. They had a real good show.

I've spent about $40 since New Year's Eve—sounds like quite a lot doesn't it—but that's just what I figured I'd spend so guess it's O.K. It takes quite a bit to eat and sleep and entertain yourself for 10 days.

Back to the old grind in a couple of days. Only this term it'll be harder because I haven't studied any of this stuff before. I wouldn't be at all surprised if I flunk out. I don't understand this electricity very well.

There was something else I wanted to tell you but I can't think of it so I'll close for now. Love, Glade

Saturday evening

Jan. 28, 1944
Bethlehem, Pa.
Dear Folks;

I've a little time to spare so guess I'd better writes to you huh?

We got a chance to see all our grades fo last term the other day. I didn't flunk anything. I made one 65, one 75, two 80s and one 90. Guess that's good enough. One half of my section flunked math so my 65 in that wasn't too bad.

We've been having quite a few tests lately. I've passed them all except the one this morning and I really messed it up. I know I didn't get over 40 on it. It was in alternating current and I've never had it before—I'd been studying hard though and thought I knew sthe stuff pretty well. Maybe I'll do better on the next one. I really do understand it fairly well.

Do you read all the stuff about breaking up A.S.T.P.? Don't hardly know what to think. No one here knows much about it. We're wondering whether well get to finish or not. If you listen to the radio you can get the idea we'll be overseas by the end of the year. I wouldn't doubt it . Air Corp. ground signal communication is open now and I might be able to get into that. Jim and I were talking of it the other day. Guess I'll go down Wednesday and see what the story is. Let me know what you think about it.

Sounds like Gene is doing pretty fair. That wasn't the school he wanted to go to tho was it?

Bob Harris sounds like he thinks he's winning the war by himself. I doubt it.

Is guess Dad will have had his birthday by the time you get this. Hope you had a happy one anyway Dad. I got a book to send but a couple of guys saw it and read it (me too) and then I put it away and forgot to mail it. I'll try to gset it in the mail soon.

Not much else to say, I'm afraid. Love, Glade
Pfc. Glade Lyon—Co. C 3309 S.U.—Bethlehem, Pa.

Sunday afternoon

Feb. 7, 1944
Bethelem, Pa.
Dear Folks,

Haven't much to say but guess I'd better write a letter to let you know I'm still alive.

Last week was the fourth week of this term. We always have a lot of tests the fourth week so I'm glad it's over. I think I passed all the tests tho.

Gee, I've been in the army eight months. Pretty good huh? Seems like years since I was home tho.

A bunch of us went to the show "Phantom Lady" last night. It was pretty good. We had quite a lot of fun.

I can't find your last letter so I'll have to wait until I do to answer any questions you asked.

Mildred says she's planning to go to the University next fall. She was thinking of going into the Cadet Nurse Corp. but I guess I and her folks talked her out of that.

Guess I'll go down to the U.S.O. for a while tonite. There doesn't seem to be much else to do. Next Saturday we're having a big Military Ball that'll be a lot of fun. Two orchestras and all the trimmings.

Our schedule as been changed a little here. We have free time until eight-thirty instead of seven-thirty every night. That's nice sometimes but it makes for less studying.

Feb. 14th is Valentine's Day again. Also is date of my first date with Mildred. It' been just two years since we met.

I hope Daddy had a nice birthday. I'm going to send the book and some old copies of "Yank" I've been saving. Maybe they'll be interesting.

I guess I'd better close. I've been an hour writing this and haven't said anything yet. Love, Glade
Pfc. Glade Lyon—Co. C 3309 S. U.- Bethlehem, Pa,

Wednesday noon

Feb. 9, 1944
Bethlehem, Pa.
I've been thinking it over for quitse a while and decided to put in my application. Jim is too. Since I'm under 21, you have to sign it. I also have to send three letters of recommendation & birth certificate & transcript of college credits. I wrote Mr. Hess, Mr. Meikle, and Tom Murdoch for the letters and I sent for the transcript. I already have the birth certificate. Maybe you'd ask either Rulon or Lup or somebody for a letter of recommendation for me in case one of the others don't come through huh?

Well O.K. Thanks

Everythings O.K. here. Studying pretty hard. But I flunked my first quiz the other day. Oh well—Gotta rush. Love, Glade

Pfc. Glade Lyon—Co. C 3309 S.U.—Bethlehem, Ps.

Sunday afternoon

Feb. 14, 1944
Bethlehem, Pa.
Dear Folks.
Will, her it is letter writing time again. Last week went about as usual except that I flunked a quiz but so did almost every one else so guess it's not too awful bad. Bad enough though.

It started snowing about Thursday and we have about six or eight inches of snow on the ground now. That's quite a lot for this part of the country I guess. The sun is shining today but it's still fairly cold.

The Regimental Ball was last night. It was quite an affair. Two good local orchestras. They picked the queen of the Ball and had a grand marshall and everything. We had a lot of fun. There were five couples of us that went together. Jim & Margy, Margee & I, "Brad" and Marge, Doug and Dot, & Katy and Gus. Guess you don't know who most of them are. Maybe I can explain a little. There are five girls in this one bunch who are usually together. Margee and Fran Bedics, Marge and Dot Ardle, and Katherine Trimble. They're all pretty swell girls. All attractive and have nice personalities and all go with A.S.T.'s here at Lehigh so we have some pretty good times together. Margee & Dot are 19 and the others are all 20, I think. It's sort of confusing having three girls in one crowd named Margaret though. We try to get around it by calling my girl "Marjy," Jim's wife "Margy," and the other one "Marj" but we get mixed up sometimes.

Guess I'll go down to the show and then over to the U.S.O. for awhile. Don't seem to have much to write about lately.

I'm going to try to get that book in the mail this week but I dunno. Love, Glade

Pfc. Glade Lyon—Co. C 3309 S. U.—Bethlehem, Pa.

Feb. 21, 1944

Bethlehem, Pa.
Dear Folks,

I just got your telegram. But maybe they've already decided for me whether or not I should go into the Ground Crew. It was closed about three days ago. And I still haven't received two of the letters of recommendation I needed before I could turn in my application. It looks now as though they'll be kicking me out of A.S.T. soon anyway. Kaltenborn says A.S.T. will be cut to 35,000 by April first. According to him only medical and dental students will be left. But the Philadelphia paper said engineers would also stay—but I doubt it very much. The setup now is that anyone flunking one course at the end of the eighth week of the term will be removed. And I'm afraid that'll be me. We have a lab course that we only get one quiz in each four weeks. On the first one I got 46 so I'll have to do pretty good on the next one and I'm afraid I'll mess it up. As to the Air Corp.—I think I should have turned in my application. It would be a better deal than A.S.T.P. I think. We would have received some school there and the chance of a commission or rating would be much better. I'm afraid we'll be a long time getting ratings from A.S.T.P.

Didn't I ever thank you for the pictures? I sure meant to. It seems like I did but maybe not. I sure do like them anyway. They're about the best pictures I've ever seen of you folks.

Didn't do much last night. The town ws pretty dead. Saw "Lost Angel"—a darn good show—and then went over to the Elks Club for awhile.

Did I tell you I was getting my teeth fixed? I had one small cavity and one large one. The army paid for it and one of the local dentists did the work.

Since A.S.T. is closing—maybe—I don't know whether I'll get a furlough or not. We had several classes last week so I didn't have a chance to find out about fare or route to K.C. I'll try and do it this week. If we do get our furloughs I imagine they'll start April 1 or 2.

I bought a $25.00 bond during the 4th Drive but I guess I shouldn't have done it. I'm running pretty short of money on account of it. I think I can get by. If I can't, I'll send you an S.O.S. next month. I'll sell you the bond for $10.00 or something like that. Oh well, we shall see.

Can't think of anything else to say so I'll call a halt to it. Love, Glade.

Pfc. Glade M. Lyon—Co. C—3309 S. U.—Bethlehem, Pa.

Sunday afternoon

Feb. 28, 1944
Bethlehem, Pa/
Dear Folks,
Well here it is Sunday again. The time sure flies by. The weather is all sloppy again. First it snows and then as soon as that has all melted, it snows, again. Very discouraging.

Sunday afternoon

You said for me to promise to answer all your questions and then you only asked about two—so I guess I can do that.

Of course I want to meet you in Kansas City. But I'm beginning to be afraid I won't get to. I just don't know. Everything is so uncertain. Lehigh is to have 200 to 300 A.S.T.'s here next term but whether we'll be among them or not is something no one seems to know. And besides that, I may flunk out. That is a distinct possibility. In either case, I have no assurance of a furlough in April. I rather expect one but I'm not too sure. I still haven't found out about train or plane fare or routes. But I'll find out tomorrow for sure and let you know soon.

Had a few quizzes last week but I guess I did O.K. on them.

Went to the show last night. It was pretty darned good. Name of "A Guy Named Joe" with Spencer Tracy. Margee called up this morning and asked me over for dinner this evening so I'll have to start getting ready soon.

I'm working myself up into quite a problem here. Maybe you can tell me what to do. It's Margee & Mildred. I decided several months ago that I sure wasn't ready to start thinking of betting married and I was wishing that I wasn't engaged to Mildred. I've changed a lot since I left Idaho and right now I doubt if I'll ever want to go back to Moscow after the war. I'll probably be doing a lot of wandering around like everyone else. At any rate, I wrote Mildred a couple of months ago and told her that I thought we ought to call it off, but she didn't think so. Now I've been going with Margee quite awhile and I'm getting so I like her a lot. It's not hardly fair to Mildred I'm afraid. I'd like to break the engagement and just be very good friends with Mildred but I don't know whether I should just write and break it up like that or not. I could sure use some good advice. How about it? I'm afraid we'll never make a go of it anyway so it'd probably be best to break now. But I don't know what to do.

Well, it's a quarter of 4 and I'm to be at Margee's in an hour so guess I'd better go shave. Love, Glade

Pfc. Glade Lyon—Co. C 3309 S. U.—Bethlehem, Pa.

Saturday afternoon

Mar. 4, 1944
Bethlehem, Pa.
Dear folks,
Well, here it is Saturday again and I am downhearted! It's snowing again—it does every Saturday—and too, I just finished my third & last quiz of the day. And I'm afraid I only passed one of the. I'm pretty sure I flunked the only one that really matters so I'll probably be leaving Lehigh soon.

About train schedules—I still haven't found out. It's quite aways down to the depots and I don't very often have time. I called a couple of times but I couldn't get any information that was though. I did find out about plane service. Fare is $55.50 or thereabouts, one way—so that's out of the question. Good time though. Leave here a little after 4 P.M. and in Kansas City by 11:00.

We get off every night from 6 until 8:30 now. Jim & Margy and Margee & I went to the show about Wednesday night and Jim & I just barely got back here in time to shout "here" when they called out our names at formation. They don't usually have a formation at 8:30, but they pull one every once in a while to see who they can catch. So we were almost restricted for the weekend—but not quite—so it's O.K.

The four of us were planning to go to New York today, but we decided to wait until next Saturday.

That bond—I paid cash for it, but after I wrote you I started thinking I was going to be pretty short so I sold it to Jim & Margy. So now I'm pretty flush. The trip to New York will be pretty expensive though so I'll probably need it. Thanks a lot for sending the check. I may not need it but I probably will for the trip to New York. So if you don't mind and don't need it too bad, I'll keep it. I'll try to repay you sometime not too far away. I sort of want to go to New York because I've only been there once and I may be shipped to some other part of the country soon.

Did I tell you I as over to Margee's for supper last Sunday? Fran's fellow (from a camp in Maryland) was up and we had a good time. Went to the U.S.O. after we ate.

Guess we'll go to a show tonight. There's not much else to do it seems. There's another Regimental Ball coming up, on the 18th I believe. Margee & I had a picture taken at the other Ball. I'm going to wrap that stuff I've been threatening to send you and I'll put it in the book. It's a very poor picture but I thought maybe you'd like to see it and get a little idea what she looks like.

Can't think of anything else to say so so long for now. Do whatever you like about plans for the trip to K.C. Love, Glade

I wanted to mention the soldier vote. All of us here think we got a pretty dirty deal. Congress seems to be a lot more interested in playing their little games of politics than in doing anything worth while. If you find out what Idaho intends to do about soldier voting let me know will you? I want to help kick out our two senators and put in F.D.R. as president again. He seems to be the only man in Washington more interested in the war than reelection. Glade

Pfc. Glade Lyon—Co. C 3309 A.S.T.U.—Bethlehem, Pa.

Monday night

Mar. 14, 1944
Bethlehem, Pa.
Dear Folks,

I really should be studying but I know you'll be wanting to hear from me so here goes. I haven't done much studying tonight. We've all been arguing Einstein's Theory of Relativity instead. And what we don't know about it would fill volumes.

We went to New York Saturday—Jim, Margy, Margee & I. And we sure had a lot of fun. We stayed at the Hotel Martinique. It's on Greeley Square. We intended to see a stage play but everything we wanted to see was sold out so we just wandered around for awhile and then went down to Greenwich Village (in lower Manhattan) and went to Tony Pastor's nite club for awhile. They had a good floor show. After we left there we went back to the Hotel and went to bed. Sunday morning at nine o'clock we went to mass at St. Patrick's Cathedral and then had breakfast at Child's Restaurant. Next we went up to Central Park and hired one of the little horse-drawn carriages they have there for a ride through the park. It was just like you see in the movies—the driver had on a tall black silk hat and a long black coat—and we had a lot of fun. Then we looked around the Central Park Zoo awhile. After we ate, we climbed up on top of a Fifth Avenue Bus and rode as far as it went. Up through Harlem and past Yankee Stadium and the Polo Grounds and lots of other places. Then we went back to the Hotel and checked out and took our stuff over to Penn Station and checked it. After that we took the subway down to Battery Park and looked at the ships and the Statue of Liberty awhile. Then back to Penn Station and home. I spent $30.00 but it was well worth it 'cause I really had a good time.

I passed all my quizzes so I'm still in school. But we still don't know whether we'll get furloughs or not so I don't know what to tell you. It's after taps so I'll have to close. Love, Glade

Pfc. G. Lyon—Co. C 3309 S.U.—Bethlehem, Pa.

March 20, 1944

Bethlehem, Pa.
Dear Folks,
Guess you got my telegram. It's not definite but everything points toward no furloughs. One of Jim's friends, who is taking the same course we are a George Washington U. in St. Louis, finished term 5 two weeks ago and started right into term six with no furlough. Also, if we were to get furloughs we'd have

March 20, 1944   *151*

(probably) filled out the forms two weeks ago and we still haven't. So it looks pretty doubtful.

Didn't do much this weekend. They held another Regimental Ball but it wasn't very good so we didn't stay long. Saw a show instead. Margee & I borrowed Jim's camera this afternoon and took some pictures. I'll send you a couple if they're any good.

It's been fairly nice here this past week—almost looked as if spring had come. But it turned cold again yesterday and even started to snow this evening.

I don't think taking Margee to New York was too bad. I've told Mildred that I've been going with Margee, that I like her quite a bit, and that I want to break the engagement. That seems to me to be honest enough & fair enough too.

About that bond I sold to Jim—maybe I can't do it, but I did. I had it made out to him instead of you. You see I bought it through the army and I decided to change it over to him before it was made out so it worked out O.K.

All those quizzes I was sure I flunked—I passed. I was pretty surprised. The one I was sure I flunked, I got 94 in. Amazing ain't it? I really didn't know that much about it. Just made some good guesses.

We're (Co. C) having a party tomorrow night. We've quite a bit of money in the company fund and I guess that's the best way to spend it.

Well, I've got another quiz coming up tomorrow so guess I'd better close and start studying. Love, Glade

Pfc. Glade Lyon—Co. C 3309 S. U.—Behtlehem, Pa.

Tuesday afternoon

Mar. 29, 1944
Bethlehem, Pa.
Dear Folks

Got notice of money at Western Union a little while ago so I'll go down this evening and pick it up. Thanks a million. The reason for the call of distress was the fact that I was sure we'd ship before Saturday so we won't get paid until the end of next month. I'm going to send for my bonds and cash them in and try to pay you part of what I owe you and have some for spending money.

We've been having a lot of parties and sstuff around here the last few days.

We just found out a few minutes ago that we're shipping Thursday to Fort Monmouth, N.J. It's right on the coast. The only thing there is signal corp so it sounds like it's about the best place we could be sent.

Jim, Margy, Margee, & I went to Philadelphia Sunday. We started out to rent some bikes and ride out to the country club but the bike shop was closed so we started out hitch hiking. But the people who gave us a ride were going quite a ways so we went along and then got another ride and the first thing we knew we were in Phily, so we walked around awhile, saw a show, and took the midnight train back. Lot of fun huh?

I'm sending some of the pictures we took in New York. We've been taking others lately. I'll send them as soon as they're developed. Keep them all for me until after the war will you please? I want to put them all in an album.

Oh say, when we were in New York, up on top of the Rockefeller Center, we looked in the registration book under Idaho and Kay Hammond had been there just a month before. Is he up around here somewhere?

About time for chow so I'll sign off and write again when we get settled. Love, Glade

6–24–44

Pfc. Glade Lyon—Co. C 3309 S.V.—Bethlehem, Pa.

6–24–44

Fort Monmouth, N.J.
Dear Folks,
Well, 2 days of my 3 day pass have gone already. Darn it. We've really been having a swell time. The Barbers & Margee & all came to Asbury Park and we've been laying on the beach. Were in the ocean yesterday & it was nice. Went bike riding today. Time to go eat—so long for now. Love, Margee & Glade
Pfc. G. M. Lyon—Co. F 15th S.T.R.—Fort Monmouth, N.J.

Monday noon

June 26, 1944
Fort Monmouth, N.J.
Dear Folks,
I got off a little early this morning so I'll write you a letter. It's about time huh? I finished school Thursday, so I was on detail this morning. Some of the fellows who finished Wednesday are shipping today so I imagine I'll be gone very soon.

Jim & I both took our passes Thurs. night. We met the girls in Red Bank at 7:30 PM. Margee and I went straight from there to Asbury but Jim & Margy stayed at Fort Monmouth that night and came to Asbury about noon Friday. We never did have much sunshine but it was quite warm. Friday afternoon we went in the ocean—that was the only time we did, the rest of the time it seemed too cold. Saturday morning we went out on the beach and laid around—dug holes in the sand & built a nice castle. That afternoon we rented bikes & rode over to Fort Monmouth & back (about 8 miles each way). Sat. nite we went on the boardwalk but it rained so we went back to the hotel & played cards & then went to bed. Sunday morning Jim & Margy went to New York.

Margee & I walked around the boardwalk for a while and then went to church. Went back to the hotel, ate, & started for the station. She took the 5:00 o'clock train home & I rode as far as Red Bank with her. We sure had a swell time. Spent $30.00. That's plenty but not too much. Hotel was $10.50. Main trouble was that it was over so soon.

Jim knows pretty definitely that he is to get his overseas furlough next month. It's a military secret of course but it sort of leads me to think I may get one in a month or two. When & if I do, I think I'll bring Margee along. She's such a sweet kid & I've got so I like her a lot. It's O.K. with you if she comes isn't it? I've got her saving her money so she can buy her ticket out & back.

I've been wondering how Daddy is ever since I got your letter. I sure hope he gets some better soon. Wish I could be home to help out when the going gets rough.

I've got to close & get ready to go on the training program.
Love, Glade
Pfc. Glade M. Lyon—Co. F 15th S.T.R,—Fort Monmouth, N.J.

August 8, 1944

Fort Monmouth, N.J.
Dear Folks,
I didn't even go out to the air base. I talked to an officer stationed there & he said there was no chance to catch a ride because all they had was fighters. No. 26 is late so I'll take it to Chicago.
Love, Glade
Pfc. G. M. Lyon—Co. C 3186 S.S.B

Telegram

Aug. 10, 1944
Bethlehem, Pa.
J T Lyon
Made connections okay arrived this morning Love.
Glade

Monday nite

Aug. 16, 1944
Ft. Monmouth, N.J.
Dear Folks,

I took the Pacific Limited from Pocatello. It was late—didn't leave there until 1 P.M., but we got to Chicago at 7:10 and weren't due there until 7:30, so it wasn't such a slow train after all. I had plenty of time to eat & catch my train in Chicago but we were late into Buffalo and I just barely made connections there. If I hadn't made it, I'd have had an all night layover. I got to Bethlehem at 6:48 A.M. Margee was waiting for me at the station—I wired her after I left Buffalo. I got a hotel room & cleaned up and then we looked around all day & ditto Friday. I got back to camp about 10:30 Friday nite. I thought sure I'd be on K.P. or guard duty over the weekend but they slipped up so I went to Bethlehem Saturday night. Jim was there over the weekend too and I was glad because I hadn't seen him for over a month. We went to the show Sat. nite & Sunday we went to a weiner roast.

It's awfully hot here now. Seems like I sweat constantly. And I just sleep on top of my bunk, with no covers at all.

I'm on guard duty tonite and tomorrow. I just finished 6:00 to 8:00 shift and I go back on from midnite until 2:00, then from 7:00 to 8:00 and 4:00 to 5:00 tomorrow.

All we're doing around here so far is going to classes. I think we'll be starting some of the real stuff in a few days. But I won't ever be able to tell you much about it because we have a sort of "spot check" censorship.

That's about all for now. Love, Glade

No airmail stamps & no chance to get any tonite so this'll have to go regular mail unless I can borrow one.

Pfc. Glade M. Lyon—Co. C 3186 Sig. Sv. Bn.—Ft. Monmouth, N.J.

Monday Evening

?? Aug. ?? 1944
Dear Folks.

I got your letter this morning. I also got some air mail stamps over the weekend so that'll speed things up a bit.

We haven't been doing much around here. Just classes every day. We don't have enough equipment so we can do any actual work but I hope we will have soon.

I went to Bethlehem as usual Saturday night. Jim was there, so the four of us got together and ate and then took in a late show. Sunday was a nice day but I felt so lazy that we just loafed around the house all day. I ate breakfast, dinner, & a snack in the evening there. We took a walk around campus for an hour or so in the evening & then I came back to camp.

I was thinking about our talking about whether Margee should spend more of her money when we go together. I eat at their place at least two meals every weekend. Margee almost always buys the film we use & always pays to have them developed. Several times I've left dirty suntans there & they have washed and ironed them for me. And several times Margee has handed me a dollar or two to pay for a meal or something like that. So, all in all I think it's ok don't you?

I heard Lt. Bungarda was over to the day room playing ping-pong with the fellows for beers so I came over here. I played but lost. A couple of fellows have won but not most of them.

I hope Mother had a good time in Boise. And I hope Dad is still feeling ok.

I don't know yet whether I'll get to New York on my birthday or not. I sort of doubt it but I may.

And speaking of my birthday, just forget it. Send me a box of homemade cookies or candy. If you have lots of extra money & want to get rid of it, put $5.00 in the bank for me and that'll be swell. Margee's been asking what I want & I really don't know of a thing that can be purchased now that I want. (I would like to get married—would you mind?

Guess that's about all for now. It's getting late and I'm tired. I intended to wash a lot of clothes but guess it'll have to wait until tomorrow. Love, Glade

P.S.—Margee's 20th birthday is November 15th. I'm trying to think of something for her. If you remember will you send her a card or something?

Pfc. G. M. Lyon—Co. C 3186 Sig. Sv. Bn.—Fort Monmouth, N. J.

August 30, 1944

Ft. Monmouth, N. J.

Dear Folks,

I'm on guard today so I haven't much to do. I didn't get much sleep last night 'cause I was on from midnite until three, but guess I'll catch up on that tonite.

I got your letter today. I remember talking to a lady from the bus from Rexburg to Rigby but I don't remember what she looked like. I talk to so many people that way that I don't pay much attention.

Speaking of Legion affairs—there's something I'd like you to get for me. It's a "Hospitality Card." In Easton Sat. nite we went up to the Legion Hall but they wouldn't let us in until one of the fellows flashed his Hospitality Card and then there was nothing to it. So see what you can do.

By the way, our mail is being censored now so I can't say anything about our training or equipment or plans, etc.

I met Margee in Easton last Thursday nite and we had a good time. And I went to Bethlehem Sat. nite. Some other kids from Beth, were going to Easton so we went along and had a good time. I had to leave Sun. afternoon because I had to be back in camp at 5:30 for guard duty.

Is there any place you could pick me up a very small radio? And how about a Boy Scout flashlight? Also ask Joe Klamt what kind (if any) of a camera or kodak he has for sale and let me know, will you? Thanks.

Thursday is payday so I'll be rich again instead of broke as I am now. Margee and I are going to N.Y. Sat. night and come back Sunday. I wouldn't do it except that I think I ought to celebrate my becoming a man some way or other.

Guess that's about all for now.

Oh no! Will you go down and give Ott Harris $1.50 for me? It's a lot of trouble for me to get a money order. The money is for two pocket knives for Margee's little brothers (Johnny and Mike) that I had Ott send to me. I'll send the money to you later. Thanks. Love, Glade

Pfc. G. Lyon—Co. C. 3186 Sig. Sv. Bn.—Ft. Monmouth, N.J.

Sept. 7, 1944

Thursday nite
Ft. Monmouth, N.J.

Sorry I've been so slow writing but I've been busy and lazy. I got the cookies and candy on the first. They sure were good. Thanks a lot. And thanks a lot for the bond too. I'll need it after the war.

The only other birthday present I got was a picture from Margee. I wanted one that would fit in that little album with you folks' pictures. She had one taken and colored and it fit perfectly.

Sept. 7, 1944

A week ago Monday (the one before my birthday) I got permission to get off from Friday midnite to Monday morn. But Tuesday noon they said all passes were cancelled so I forgot about it. I did get out at noon on Saturday and got Margee and we went to New York. We didn't do much but the change of scenery was nice. We went up on the Astor Roof (high society stuff) for awhile. It was very nice but too expensive so we didn't stay long. Ate at Diamond Jim's and at Lindy's. Had a good time all in all.

Thanks for the letter you wrote for my birthday. I liked it so much. I've read it several times already.

I should have written as soon I came back from N.Y. I guess but I was on K.P. until 11 pm Monday . Tuesday worked all day and took tests at night. Wednesday I was busy all day but got a letter from Margee asking me to meet her in Easton Wed. nite so I went down. So your letter got neglected.

We've finished this phase of our training now so it probably won't be too long—And that's about all I can say—"military security" you know—and our mail is being censored. I don't know anything for sure anyway.

My grandparents sent me a card with some nice thoughts written in.

Margee says they don't need the stamps at all but I'll give them to them anyway. O.K? Unless you need them.

The tests I said we took Tuesday night are ones on military matters and on our equipment. We have to pass them to get our ratings. They weren't too hard so I'm sure I passed. We may get our ratings at any time now.

Well it's time for me to hit the hay.

Thanks again for everything. Love, Glade

P.S.—Note my correct address on envelope.

Pfc. Glade Lyon—Co. C 3186 Sig. Sv. Bn.—Position 1103—Ft. Monmouth, N.J.

Saturday morning

Sep. 8, 1944 ??
Ft. Monmouth, N.J.
Dear Folks,

Yesterday I took and passed the last of my tests, so now I'm eligible for promotion. And I'd just as soon have it now as later. Don't know when I'll get it though.

We haven't had much to do this week but I guess we'll be busy from now on. This morning all of a sudden we got orders to set up our equipment for a field problem. We will be in direct communication with the two other places and the stuff will have to be worked on all the time. Each team will be on duty 48 hours at a time.

I was hoping to get out this weekend but it looks sort of doubtful with this new set-up. My team will probably be on duty.

I haven't heard yet what you thought about me being engaged, but now I've another one. Margee wants me to turn Catholic. I told her long ago that I wouldn't be a Catholic, that I wouldn't ever interfere with her going to church, and that any children of ours could be baptized into the Catholic church. And she said O.K. But now she wants me to be a Catholic. I said "no" again, but I don't know that it makes much difference. I'm quite sure that I'll never be a good member of any church so don't know as it matters much which one I am bad member of. What's your opinion? Guess that's all for now. Love, Glade

Pfc. Glade M. Lyon—Co. C—3186 Sig. Sv. Bn.—Fort Monmouth, N.J.

Sept. 12, 1944

Tuesday nite
Ft. Monmouth, N.J.
Dear Folks.

Well, let's see—what to say? Friday evening all of a sudden they told me that if I wanted to take off until Tuesday morn. to go ahead. So, never one to argue with headquarters, I rushed down to Bethlehem. We didn't do anything very exciting but it was nice to be with Margee for a few days. They were sure nice to me—as usual. I slept there, ate there & everything. And of course, they won't let me even attempt to pay them anything.

I think I'll buy Margee a ring. What do you have to say about that? Not a very expensive one because I'm not very rich, but just something to show that—something or other, I guess. You know what I mean. I know, I bought a ring once before and now I'm sorry but I think I've learned my lesson. And I think this is the real thing. (I hope.) I haven't decided definitely yet but I sort of have and I don't think I'll be sorry.

I hope everything is O.K. at home. Hope Connie likes school O.K. now. And hope your cold weather didn't make Dad worse.

We're still not doing much here. Classes and loafing are about all. We seem to be getting ready to go but it'll still be awhile yet I think.

Thanks for sending the Hospitality Card. Don't worry much about the other stuff. It's practically impossible to get. Verda's kodak wouldn't be much good for me to take overseas I'm afraid so don't ask. I'd like a 35 m.m. camera but I don't think you can buy them. And a small radio but I doubt if you can buy them either (unless second hand—which would be O.K. but it has to be tiny). That's about all for now I guess. Love, Glade

   Pfc. Glade Lyon—Co. C 3186 Sig. Sv. Bn.—Ft. Monmouth, N.J.

Tuesday nite

Sep. 19, 1944
Ft. Monmouth, N.J.
Dar Folks,

Sorry you haven't been hearing from me lately but blame it mostly on our mail service. Mail is censored here then sent to Battalion headquarters, then to Monmouth and then out. So it takes quitse awhile. Stupid isn't it? But I think I've written at least once a week.

Last Friday nite I went down to Bethlehem, bought a diamond and gave it to Margee. And I wish I had done it long ago. She was so happy she didn't know what to say or do. I've never seen anyone so tickled over anything as she was. She's really a fine girl. I'd like you to keep on writing to her after I go over, and if she needs any help or any anything, do whatever you can for her. I know you'll like her. She's such a sweet kid.

I'm glad to hear that Dad is so much better. And Pres. Hess too. And that's pretty good about Danny, huh?

Jim Graves is in New York at P.O.E., I'd sure like to see him but guess it can't be done.

We took some tests awhile back and I have one more to take tomorrow. If I make the grade on it, I'll be up for promotion. Jim Barber got his T/5 stripes a few days ago.

When I go overseas, I think I'll send some money to you and some to Margee. Is that O.K. with you? I could send it all to you but I'd like to have some of it available to her in case she should need some cash for something.

Just forget the flash, radio, etc. I can get the flash and the rest is not on the market. Thanks for trying.

I'm starting to wonder about Xmas. I haven't the slightest idea what you folks would like. I've been away too long to know your wants.

Did you read about the hurricane we had? It really wrecked

things over on the coast. About all we had was a lot of heavy rain though. Had a little trouble keeping communication lines open.

I planned to go to Bethlehem tonite but it looked pretty much like rain so I put it off until tomorrow. It didn't rain tho so now I'm unhappy.

That's about all I can think of, so I'll close for now. Love, Glade

P.S.—Margee's folks have more stamps than they know what to do with so I'm returning those you sent. Thanks anyhow.

Mom: make me a cookie sometime when you have nothing else to do. Thanks.

Pfc. Glade M. Lyon—Co. C 3186 S.S.Bn. Position 1103—Ft. Monmouth, N.J.

Wednesday

Oct. 7, 1944
Ft. Monmouth, N.J.
Dear Folks,
Seems like I just can't get around to writing you folks.

I got the cookies yesterday. Thanks a lot. They're sure good. They weren't broken up as much as usual. They're almost all gone now. The fellows have been working on them all morning.

Up until now we've just been having classes, etc. but tomorrow morning we go out in the field to set up a system. We'll probably work on it for three or four days.

I'm sorry I asked your advice about the ring and then didn't wait for it but I knew I wanted to buy it and didn't think you'd object so I might as well do it right away.

I think you got the wrong idea about my reasons for sending money to Margee. She isn't quitting work now—in fact, she's started working overtime so she can put some in the bank for us. That's pretty swell of her, huh?

P.O.E. (the place Jim Graves is) stands for Port of Embarkation. I wrote to him but didn't get an answer.

I didn't mean to get you very excited about the prospect of my leaving the church, because I don't intend to. Not very soon at any rate. Religion (the go to church on Sunday kind) doesn't mean much to me now. It may someday, I don't know. But I don't think I'll change churches unless it's necessary to keep peace in my home.

I saw Jim Barber & wife last weekend and he's a T/4. That's three stripes with a T. I'm up for T/5 now, but it hasn't come through yet. Jim was only T/5 for eleven days before he got boosted. I hope they do that to me.

I was down to Bethlehem last weekend and the one before. Just did the usual stuff—movies, etc.

Not a very long letter but I don't know what to write. Love, Glade

P.S.—I heard from Maxine Ostler the other day.

I have a small lock in drawer of chest of drawers (or maybe on handle. Send it to me huh? And send me that sweater I sent home once. Thanks.

Pfc. Glade M. Lyon—Co. C 3186 Sig. Serv. Bn.—Ft. Monmouth, N.J.

Friday, Oct. 9, 1944 [mailed with above]

Ft. Monmouth, N.J.

Dear Folks,

I didn't mail this Wednesday because I didn't have a stamp. I got your letter with one today so I'll send it now. I tried to get stamps but couldn't.

I've been very busy lately. Wed. nite I went to Beth. Because I found out that I'd be on duty over the weekend. We went on duty at the terminal here Thur. morning and we'll probably be on at least until Sun. nite. Boy they really keep me busy on that terminal. A telephone under each arm, one in each hand, and six more ringing. But it's fun.

Wed. morning

I got a letter from Winston today. I'm going to try and get a pass and then have him meet me in Beth.

I have (or used to have) two electric switches around there someplace. They look like this—(hand drawn sketch here).

If you can find them, send them to me. O.K.? Thanks.

Guess that's all. No it's not! Don't worry about me changing churches. I think I believe the Mormon is right. I do believe part of what they teach. I won't do any changing for a long time if I ever do. (Which I doubt). There is lots of time for that. Margee doesn't expect me to and I don't intend to. Let's forget it.

I think I know where I can get the Book of Mormon. I'll let you know if it falls through. Love, Glade

Pfc. Glade M. Lyon—Co.C 3186 Sig. Serv. Bn.—Ft. Monmouth, N.J.

Wed. morning

Oct. 19, 1944
Red Bank, N.J.
Dear Folks,

I got your letter Monday. I didn't write last week—couldn't find time. They kept me pretty busy. We were on terminal duty from Thur. (2 weeks tomorrow) until the following Tues. then had a pass until Thurs morn. I was on K.P. until noon Thurs day and then went to Camp Edison to fire the 50 cal. machine gun. Got back from there on Sunday and went down to Bethlehem. Monday morn. I went on guard duty and was on until last nite. Today we go on terminal duty again but at the moment we are just waiting so maybe I'll have time to dash off a note to you.

I haven't seen Winston yet but perhaps I will in a few days. I wrote him once and talked to him by phone. He was going to meet me in Beth. last Wednesday but he couldn't make it.

Don't know when we'll be moving out but it looks like a month or so yet. Jim Barber will probably be going in a very few days.

If the key to that lock isn't in the drawer or else in that little porcelain dish, then I'm afraid I don't know where. Don't worry about it.

I didn't get the package yet. Guess it'll arrive today.

Margee said she hadn't heard from you for a long time. I hope you're not angry with her about that church stuff. She didn't try to get me to change or anything. She said she didn't care.

That's about all for now I guess. Love, Glade

If you're looking for a Xmas present for me, a subscription to Reader's Digest would be welcome. Also (maybe?) "Astounding Stories." It's a science fiction mag. By Street and Smith I think.

Pfc. Glade M. Lyon—Co. C 3186 Sig. Serv. Bn.—Ft. Monmouth, N.J.

Monday nite

Oct. 23, 1944
Fort Monmouth, N. J.
Dear Folks,

I haven't written for awhile but the reason is that we have been out in the field. And that ain't all—we still are. This is a teletype machine I am writing on now, in case you were wondering. We are at a little camp down in central Jersey. We came down last Thursday and we are going back home about this coming Thursday I guess. It isn't bad down there except that it is rather cold and I mean rawther!

There are six men on my team but two of have to be on duty all the time so we took our six shelter halves and made one four man tent (twice as long as usual) to sleep in and one regular size pup tent for our bags and other equipment. We fixed it up pretty nice for sleeping purposes. We got hold of four mattresses and put them on the ground, then we hooked in the electricity we have to have for our system and got power for a light bulb and a radio.

Monday nite 167

We also hooked up a telephone so we could call from the tent to the radio tent or to the telephone terminal. Pretty slick huh?

They brought our first mail since Thursday down today and I got a letter and package from you. Thanx for the pkg although the sweater is the only thing I need. I'll send the rest back with the other stuff I have that I don't need.

Hope dad got all the deer he wanted. I'm glad he got to go, but I hope the bad weather didn't make him sick. There are quite a few deer around this part of the country. Too bad we don't have any ammunition.

I got a Book of Mormon from Salt Lake the other day so you can scratch that from off your list. I could maybe use two or three pair of the socks but I don't know what else to tell you. I need a pen (I lost mine some time ago), a watch strap and a flash light; but I think Margee is not on the trail of them. One thing I would like is some information on what I could get for you folks. I'm beating my brains out trying to think of something. As for anything for me for Xmas just forget it. If you have money to spend, just bank it for me. I'm pretty sure I'll need the money after the war much more than I need anything now.

I haven't had a chance to see Winston yet, but I've sure been trying. I was over to Fort Dix for a couple of hours this morning and I tried to find him but couldn't. I did leave a message for him to call me tho and he did. I talked to him for a few minutes and tried to make arrangements to see him this weekend but I'm not sure enough whether I'll be able to get away to make very definite plans about anything. I suppose I'll see him sooner or later tho if I keep trying.

I guess that's enough for now. It looks like quite a letter. Love, Glade

P.S.—This is Friday morn. We got back yesterday afternoon. We get a pass starting noon today until Monday morn. That's pretty good but not too much considering we've missed the last four weekends & we're going to miss next one too.

Gotta shave and shower so I'll be ready to go. Love, Glade

Monday nite

Nov. 1, 1944
Ft. Monmouth, N.J.
Dear Folks,
Well, my pass is over and I'm back in camp. I had from Friday noon until Monday morn. Off. Had a lovely time. Slept until 11 every morning and went to a movie every nite.

Margee's birthday is the 15th but I didn't know if I'd be able to see her then so Saturday we went shopping and she picked out a week end bag and we got it. And then I picked out a fountain pen and she paid for it for my birthday. I was sure broke after I bought her the bag. It was $17.50 and I had $18.50. It's a lot of money but it was something she needed so I figured it was O.K.

The hills are surely pretty here. They are covered with trees (mostly oak & maple) and the colors are really something to see. I thot the hills around home were colorful in the fall but they can't be compared with this.

I still haven't seen Winston. I sent him a telegram that I would be in Bethlehem over the weekend and to come if he could be he didn't show up.

As far as a deer rifle for Dad, the best thing we have is the old Springfield. The same one they used in the last war. This carbine is a nice weapon but it's only good for about 200 to 300 yards and I don't imagine that's enough range for him. It just uses a plain peep sight and it's not adjustable.

What should I get Connie for Xmas. The comb-brush-mirror set? Or what? You folks probably won't get anything from me. Do you mind? I don't have much cash and I certainly don't have any idea what to get you. Let's you not get me anything and I'll get the same for you, huh?

Can't think of anything more to say so—- Love, Glade

P.S.—You asked when I'm going overseas and to that I can truthfully say that I haven't the slightest idea. Maybe next week, maybe next year.

The EF-15 is designation for type and number of my team. It's put there so that the team officers (who do the censoring) can tell which letter was written by the members of which team. Or something like that.

Pfc. Glade M. Lyon—Co, C 3186 Sig. Serv. Bn.—Fort Monmouth, N.J.

Nov. 2, 1944

Bethlehem, Ps.
Dear Folks;
I'm down to Beth. tonite. Just a quick note to let you know that we seem to be getting ready to go. A week or two yet before we get on the boat I guess. We've been getting our stuff ready so it won't be long.

I'll send a box of stuff home tomorrow if I can. Love, Glade
Next is Nov. 3
From Margee
Dear Mrs. Lyon,
I'm glad to hear that you and Connie had a nice visit and happy to hear about the buck Mr. Lyon had. Glade told me he caught two deer. I'm enclosing a little note Glade wrote last while he was up. Well it looks like he's about ready to go. Just the other day he was telling me they were going to set up more equipment and be around for a least two months. And just yesterday afternoon they tore down all the equipment and had an inspection. He brought a few of his things up which he couldn't take along when he goes (overcoat, his big hat, and a pair of trousers) so I'm almost certain he'll be leaving shortly.

Glade was talking to a civilian from Hackettstown and he told Glade that they were leaving this Tuesday (7th). Glade said civilians around an army post usually know when they're leaving before the soldiers themselves know. We're certainly going to miss him. He was just like one of the family and we all had loads of fun when he came up.

I've been waiting all evening for Glade but I guess he won't get up tonight. He said he'll be up this Saturday tho.

I don't feel much like writing so I hope you won't mind if I cut this short.

Oh! I almost forgot Glade told me to tell you not to worry about him cause he'll be alright and I'll wire you as soon as I know he's gone. So long for now, Sincerely, Margee

Nov. 16, 1944

Fort Monmouth, N. J.
Dear Folks,

I can't remember when I wrote to you last, but I suppose it's been quite awhile anyway. The same old hustle & bustle going on around here. And that's about the limit of what I can tell you. But you can never tell what'll happen next.

Yesterday was Margee's birthday. So I went down to see her. One of my buddies from camp went with me & dated Dot Ardle. We had a good time for a few hours. Thanks for sending Margee a birthday card. She said—just a second while I get her letter and I'll copy what she said -. She mentions receiving the card & letter from you & says "It made me feel so good all day." So I'm glad you sent it.

I guess I'm pretty much in love 'cause it seems about all I do is try to make her happy.

I just happened to think, Margee wanted you to send her the pictures we took while I was home. Will you have some made & send them? Thanx a lot.

Do you remember that rifle belt I sent home quite awhile ago? If Dad isn't using it for hunting or something, I wonder if it would be much trouble for you to send it to Margee's brother Johnny? He's the youngest of the family (11 years) and he's quite crazy about army equipment or anything that has to do with the army. He likes me a lot so I try to get the things he wants for him.

I've had a little cold the last few days but I think I'll have it whipped pretty soon. The weather's been pretty cold lately and when it isn't cold it's raining.

I told you about the weekend bag I got Margee for her birthday didn't I? But did I tell you we are starting a record collection so we can play our favorite tunes after the war? Bedics haven't a record player so it looks sort of foolish if you don't know the idea behind it. I've always wanted a record player & lots of records & when I found that Margee felt the same I decided we might as well get started and then when the war is over & they reconvert we can get something to play them on.

I left your last letter in Bethlehem, so if there were any questions asked, they'll have to wait until I see the letter again.

I'm glad to see my kid sis is so darn smart. I wish I was smart like that.

Well, I guess that's enough for now. I've about run out of stuff to say. Love, Glade

Pfc. Glade M. Lyon—Co. C 3186 Sig Serv Bn—Fort Monmouth, N. J.

Tuesday nite

Nov. 21, 1944
Ft. Monmouth, N.J.
Dear Folks,

I'm at the U.S.O. now. Just trying to pass away the time. I've even started knitting myself a scarf. Pretty good huh? Margee's sister Helen taught me to knit so I bought a couple of needles & some yarn and started in. I have about 1 ½ inches done, and I just started last nite. It won't be exactly a masterpiece cause I've made a lot of mistakes already, but it'll be warm I guess.

I was down to Bethlehem over the weekend again. Went to a show & layed around, as usual. We don't do much but I sure enjoy myself. By the way, do you have any idea what I could get Mr. & Mrs. Bedics for Xmas? They've been awfully good to me & I'd like to give them something.

Mrs. Bedics was sick this weekend. It's the first time I've ever seen her that way. She had a touch of rheumatism or something. Just as long as she was working, she was ok but she couldn't sit down or sleep.

Mr. & Mrs. Young, who run an ice cream parlor here in town have invited Tom McComb, Keith Hardy, & myself for turkey dinner Thursday nite. They're such nice people.

Don't know what to get Connie for her birthday. It's really got me baffled, (partly because I'm so broke).

I got a letter from Grandma and Grandpa today.

I've got a flock more stuff I should send home but guess I'll just keep it as long as I can & then throw it away. Mostly junk anyway.

Margee wants some of those pictures. (And by the way, thanks for sending them.) Send the ones of all the men & all the women, the one of the house & Connie & I, & the one of Connie alone. O.K.? Thanks! If you want, send her the negatives and she can have them made. We took some pictures Sunday evening, some of them in the house. I don't know whether they'll be any good or not but I hope so.

So you have six inches of snow? A little early for so much isn't it? Or am I forgetting? It's been snowing here today so we have about an inch of slush. Just enough to be disgusting. That's about all for now. Love, Glade.

Dad;

That sporting goods store sounds ok. Should be a money-making proposition. Don't know what Margee would think about living in Ashton though. It might not thrill her too much. But then, you never can tell. Don't know whether it'd be a good idea for me to go back to school in engineering if I was to go into that sort of business though. Maybe I should take a year of business.

I can get money on the G.I. Bill of Rights to help start a business like that too. It wounds good to me Dad. I'll probably see Margee tomorrow night & I'll see what she has to say. I'm thinking maybe a few phonograph records would go well too. What say? Glade

Or some radios. Or do you have competition in that field?

Pfc. Glade Lyon—Co. C 3186 Sig. Serv. Bn.—Ft. Monmouth, N. J.

Pfc. Glade M. Lyon

Co. C 3186 Sig. Serv. Bn.
APO 17604 % PM NY NY
Dear Folks,

I'm now "somewhere on the east coast," as you probably already know. That's about all I can tell you concerning my location or what I'm doing.

I've been going to write for the past couple of days but just couldn't seem to find time.

I'm pretty tired right now. I was on guard last night & today & then I worked in supply tonite.

This isn't a bad camp—although I'll be glad when we leave. We keep pretty irregular hours but the food is very good. The best I've ever had in the army.

Margee picked out a dresser set for Connie & she'll send it to her for Xmas so you needn't worry about it. I sure don't know what to get her for her birthday tho.

I got off about 1 pm Thanksgiving and so got to Bethlehem in time for dinner with the Bedics family. They waited for me to show up before they ate. They've certainly been nice to me since Margee and I started going together.

By the way, did you ever send that bill to Johnny? If not, don't bother because I was able to get him one. Or did I ever tell you to send it to him? I've forgotten.

I'm having Margee send home a pair of shoes for me. Dad may be able to use them if he wants to.

I guess that's all for now. I'm so tired I can't think. I'll write again soon. Love, Glade

P.S.—I'm still all for that sporting goods store. I asked Margee if she'd like to live in Ashton & she said sure. But the more she thot about it the less sure she was. I'm afraid she wouldn't find it very exciting. But I think she'll be content for a few years (more or less) there. I think we'll try it if you folks want to. Jobs are apt to be pretty scarce by the time I get out of the army. Glade

Pfc. Glade M. Lyon—Co. C 3186 Sig. Serv. Bn.—APO % PM NY NY

Dec. 17, 1944

Liverpool, England
Dear Folks,

I'm now somewhere in England. [Next line censored out.] We've been here a few days but I've been too busy to write and have been hoping for a chance to cable you.

We had a pretty good trip over. We were in a fairly small ship in a medium sized convoy.

We're in a pretty nice camp now. We're in two story brick buildings with steam heat. We have four men to a room.

I haven't had any mail since I left the states but I guess we'll get some soon. I hope I get a big box of cookies for Xmas.

I guess it will be Xmas by the time you get this. I hope you have a nice one. And I hope Connie gets everything she wants. If she doesn't, let me know and I'll see what I can do. Let me know about your Christmas won't you?

Take note of my new address (APO 507).

It's sure strange to drive on the left side of the street, and count my money in pounds, schillings and pence. But not bad after you're used to it. Write soon. Love, Glade

T/5 Glade M. Lyon—Co.C 3186 Sig. Sv. Bn.—APO 507 %PM NY NY

Jan. 4, 1945

Written Dec. 23, 1944
Liverpool, England
Dear Folks,
I made T/4 yesterday. That's sergeant to you I guess. The stripes look like this: That's a pretty good Christmas present huh?

I got my first mail this morning. A package from Margee. Maybe some more will be close on its heels.

We had eight hour passes yesterday starting at 1:00 pm. Went into town and looked the fair city over and did a little shopping. There's not too much to buy tho.

Write to me V-MAIL part of the time. It's a little faster. Guess that's all for now. Love, Glade

T/4 Glade M. Lyon—Co. C 3186 S. S. B.—APO 507 % PM NY NY

Jan. 8, 1945

Liverpool, England
Dear Folks,
Haven't written you for a couple of days. Doesn't ever seem to be much to say. What few things of interest we do I'm not allowed to write about so it's kind of hard.

I haven't got the boxes you sent yet but guess they'll show up soon. You've asked about the magazines I had you subscribe to for me. I got one copy of "Astounding" before we went to P.O.E. but that's all so far. I guess they'll catch up to me eventually. Our mail is still pretty messed up.

Thanks for the magazines for Christmas, and thanks especially for the War Bond. You don't need to send me the numbers tho. I lose the slip that I write them on almost as fast as I make it.

I'm glad Dad liked the boots. I guess you were a little surprised at the style though.

I'm sorry to hear that everyone is bsreaking up around home. Eugene & Regena and Hale & Erma. That's not good. Guess I'd better write Eugene & Regena & see what the trouble is.

"Mac" and I went in to the Red Cross last nite and watched the people dance for awhile. I met a girl (Red Cross Volunteer) from Rigby, Idaho. Pretty close to home. She knows Rhea Johnson so that's one friend we have in common at least.

It's getting late and I have to get up early tomorrow so I'll close for now. Write often. Letters mean an awful lot over here. You should see the stampede when someone says "Mail Call."
Love, Glade

Sgt. Glade M. Lyon Co. C 3186 Sig. Serv. Bn.—A.P.O. 507 % PM NY NY

Jan. 1, 1945

Postmarked Jan. 13, 1945
Liverpool, England
Dear Folks,
Happy New Year!

I don't expect to have an especially happy one myself so I'm hoping that 1946 will bring you and Margee & myself all together so we can be happy enough to make up for 43 and 44 and 45.

I stayed in camp last night and today. I have a bad cold and the weather is very damp so sI didn't think it was wise to go out.

We've been doing a lot of guard duty and standing around in the cold has given almost every one a cold.

I saw a good stage play "Cinderella" a couple of days ago and also one a couple of days before that. The opera season is over

here but they have quite a few good plays on. That's really about all there is to do in town.
Write often. Love, Glade
Sgt. Glade Lyon—Co. C 3186 S.S.B.—APO 507 % PM NY NY

Jan. 2, 1945

Postmarked Jan. 13
Liverpool, England
Dear Folks.
Just received your letter of the 11th and I was certainly glad to hear from you. I still haven't received any mail from Margee except the package.

You said in your letter that it seemed a long time since you had heard from me but I guess you had quite a wait after that because we were still at sea at that time.

I haven't received the package you mentioned but I imagine they'll be coming. If I want anything I'll ask for it but I don't know what it would be right now.

I'm sorry I didn't send Connie anything for her birthday. I hope she got the set for Christmas O,K. Margee was to buy it and send it.

Guess that's about all I have to say. I'll send you a money order for $25.00 in a day or so, Love, Glade
Sgt. Glade M. Lyon—Co. C 3186 S.S.B.—% PM NY NY

Jan. 3, 1945

Liverpool, England
Dear Folks,
Well, I finally hit the jackpot as far as mail is concerned. I guess it's starting to catch up. One from you, one from Winston and five from Margee. Your letter was dated Nov. 29th.

Glad to hear Joe Rankin is O.K. I told you Jim Barber is in

France now didn't I? And Boinest (an old buddy from Lehigh) is here in England.

I'm pretty tired right now. Went on guard from 5 P.M. to midnite last nite. Was guarding a warehouse in town so by the time I got relieved and back to camp it was 2:45. Went to sleep & had to get up at 4:00 to eat and go back on guard at 5:00 this morn. Got back to camp at 2:30 this afternoon. So you can see they keep me busy once in awhile.

I'm enclosing a money order for $25.00. That's not too much but there are a few things I need to buy so I'll hang on to the rest of it. I'll send more next month I think.

Can't think of anything more to say.

Oh yes I can. Margee said she sent Connie a bracelet for her birthday. I'm glad to hear that. I asked her to try to get something but I didn't know what so I didn't really expect her to get anything. I hope Connie liked the bracelet. In case you want to cable me for any reason just send it to: T/4 Glade M. Lyon
AMFUNI
(and I think) London, Eng.

Guess Dad will know if it is sent to London. Love to all, Glade
Sgt. Glade M. Lyon—Co. C 3186 S. S. B.—APO 507 % PM NY NY

Feb. 9, 1945

Mr. and Mrs. A. C. Miner
Dear Folks,

I got the letter and the package from you a few days ago. Thanks a lot. The cookies and nuts were swell but they didn't last long enough.

We don't do much of anything around here except details and guard duty. Not very exciting work but maybe we'll be doing the sort of work we're trained for soon.

We get passes quite frequently, but usually only for a few hours.

I did get (censored) hours a couple of weeks ago tho which gave me a chance to see London.

The English people all seem to be quite dissatisfied with things over here. I was quite surprised to find that practically every Englishman I've talked to wants to go to America after the war. They seem to think we have better government, better army, better everything. Hope to hear from you more often. Love, Glade

Sgt. Glade M. Lyon—Co. B 3186 S.S.B.—A.P.O. 407 %PM NY, NY

Undated

Restricted Certificate
[Probably Weisbaden, Germany]
#1. I certify that I have personally examine the items of captured enemy military equipment (mailed by) G. M. Lyon, that the trophy value of such items exceeds any training, service, or salvage value: that they do not include any explosives, and that the (mailing) thereof is in conformity with the provision of Sec III, Cir 353, WD, 31 Aug 1944 and the existing regulations of the Theater Commander.

#2. I further certify that the items mailed do not include any firearms capable of being concealed on the person, or any parts of firearms

#3. The items referred to are:
1—German Rifle (Mauser)
1—Bayonet
3—Ammo Pouch
1st. Lt. Will G. Mason
3186 S. S. Bn

Interesting part of this is that I packed it, completely torn down, in a wooden box along with several rounds of (prohibited) ammunition, but when it got home the end of the box and the ammunition was missing. I later traded this rifle to Bob Bean for my M1-Carbine (same model I carried all over Europe).

April 5, 1945

[Had to be Saarbrucken]
Germany
Dear Folks,
Guess it's high time I wrote you another letter. Even tho there isn't to much to say. Our work here is purely sitting and watching a couple of pieces of eletrical apparatus and answering the phone when it rings. That & getting meals and cleaning up seems to take a lot of time tho.

This city is pretty well knocked down. It's a rather hard to find a building that hasn't been it at least once. So we spend most of our free time looking at the ruins. I found a pretty good plate camera the other day (or did I tell you?) And last night I found a pair of 6x30 binoculars so I'm doing ok for myself.

Hope you're all okay. Love, Glade
Sgt. Glade M. Lyon—Co. B 3186 Sig. Sv. Bn.—APO 655 %PM NY NY

April 29, 1945

Germany
Dear Folks,
Well, I've moved again. I'm down off the mountain now. We have fifteen men of our 24 man team back together again. They've been scattered all over Germany but form some reason they've brought our team back together. It sure is good to get back with the gang again. Part of us are living in a house and part in a tent. We do our cooking and most of our living in the tent. Four of us have a van that we've got full of our equipment and we're

May 5, 1945

busy installing it. Switchboards and all sorts of stuff. We even have fluorescent lights.

I'm sure surprised to head Floyd is married. I knew he'd gone with the gal a couple of times but I sure didn't expect him to get married.

I'm working with the 12th Army Group which is composed of the 1st, 3rd, 9th and 15th Armies.

I got a package from Grandma & one from Velda today. Love, Glade

Sgt. Glade M. Lyon—Co. B 3186 S.S.B.—APO 655—%PM NY NY

May 5, 1945

Germany
Dear Folks,

I've been pretty busy the last few days so haven't had time to write. We've moved down from the radio we were guarding and we're back in the van. We've been hooking up equipment and fastening everything down so it won't get busted up when and if we move. And it's been quite a job. The trouble now is that we've still got plenty to do and the fellows with the tools we've been borrowing are moving ot. Don't know what we'll use now.

Haven't had any mail for about a week so I'm hoping it'll come thru soon. I got a package from grandma and one from Velda about a week ago. Or did I tell you?

Not much to talk about. Love, Glade

Sgt. M. Lyon—Co. B. 3186 S.S>B.—APO 655 %PM NY NY–

May 6, 1945

Germany
Dear Folks,
Just got mail again finally. But two letters only—both from you tho.

You asked about the money I am sending home. I think you had better put about everything I send home from now on in a savings account for me. Bonds are o.k. but I'm going to want some ready cash when I get home so a bank will probably be best.

We are working for the 12th Army Group. We had a circuit from them to 3rd Army for awhile but now we are running two circuits, one to 1st^{t} Army and one to 7th. But that is just what I am doing. As far as I know, this battalion is supplying communications for almost every army in the E.T.O.

I think we'll go to the C.B.I. soon after this war is over. Via the states (I hope). If we do, and we get the furlough on the way to C.B.I. I think I'll stop off in Penna. and get married. Any objection? Overruled! Love, Glade

Sgt. Glade M. Lyon—Co. B 3186 S.S.B.—APO 655 %PM NY NY

May 8, 1945

Germany
Dear Folks,
Tomorrow is officially VE Day. So I imagine everyone at home is having a big celebration at home. But there is quite a different attitude. The war is over—so what? All we want to know is when do we get home. And not just on the way to the C.B.I. but for good. Right now it appears to be quite a way in the future.

We're sure living in a crazy manner. I guess it's because we're working shifts and each day we start four hours later. But right now the majority of us go to bed about 5 or 6 in the morning and get up about 4 pm. Crazy schedule huh? We had supper tonight at 2 pm It's six am May 9 right now and I'm going to bed as soon as I sign my name to this. Love, Glade

Sgt. Glade M. Lyon—Co. B 3186 S. S. B.—APO 655—%PM NY NY

May 22, 1945

Dear Folks,
We're still here in Suchteln running this circuit for the British. It's not bad. We live in tents but we have very good food and lots of time off. We work eight hours and have 24 off (we're thinking of changing so will work 24 and have 72 off but haven't done it yet).

Didn't make it to Holland yet. I didn't go with the fellows the other days. They said it looks just like Germany tho so guess it's not important.

I called Jim Barber on the telephone last night. He is down in Marseilles. He's been transferred from 3188 to 3160 S.S.B. and says he's going to be part of the army of occupation. I wish I knew what is going to happen to us. Love, Glade

Sgt. Glade M. Lyon—Co. B 3186 S.S.B.—APO 655 % PM NY NY

June 1, 1945

Deutchland
Dear Folks,
Got more mail yesterday form you and from Margee and you both say you're not getting any mail from me. I'm sure I don't know why because I write to you folks at least every four days and sometimes oftener.

Guess Margee told you she finished her Nurses Aide coursr didn't she? I'm naturally quite proud of her.

Tell Lloyd hello for me and ask him how he does it. I'd sure like to get home for awhile.

I'm very anxious to hear more about the store. Can't you keep both Fridgidaires and Philco? How about stoves? Hotpoint ?

I hear a rumor we're coming home in September to be discharged. And another that we're going to the C.B.I. soon. I'm more inclined to believe the latter.

How's fishing Dad? Love, Glade

Sgt. Glade M. Lyon—Co. B 3186 S.S.B.—AP.O. 655 %PM NY NY

June 11, 1945

Weisbaden, Germany ?

Dear Folks,

I've been back here to battalion headquarters for about three days now. We've really been having a good time. Almost all of the battalion is back together now and everyone has stories to tell. All the places they've been and the things they've done. From Brenner Pass to Brussels. And there is plenty to drink if you want it—wine, champagne, or cognac.

I sent a package home yesterday with a chess set and a whole flock of odds and ends in it. Including a small statuette I thot Boyd might like.

I haven't received any mail for about two or three weeks from you and I'm anxious to find out how you're coming with the store. Love, Glade

Sgt. Glade M. Lyon—Co. B. 3186 S,S,B,—APO 655 %PM NY NY

July 10, 1945

Arles, France

Dear Folks,

I've been neglecting to write to you for a couple of weeks now and I'm pretty much ashamed of myself. Have been fairly busy tho. We're living in tents so have no light to write after dark and don't seem to be able to get around to writing during the day.

We're here (censored) but I couldn't tell you where to even if I knew.

I've been able to get into Marseilles three or four times on pass and had some good talks with Jim Barber.

Hope all O.K. at home. I'll write more soon. Love, Glade

Sgt. Glade M. Lyon—Co. B. 3186 Sig. Sv. Bn.—APO 655 %PM NY NY

18 July 1945

Marseille, France
Dear Sis,
Thanks for your letter. I'll try to get around to answer it one of these days.

Marseille is a pretty nice town. It's the second largest city in France. But this camp is not so good. We have to live in tents and dust gets all over everything. It's really hot here. Love, Glade

Sgt. G. M. Lyon—Co. B 186 S.S.B.—APO 655—% PM NY NY

Written Aug. 2, 1945

Postmarked Aug. 27, 1945
Censored V-Mail
At sea
Dear Folks,
We've been at sea for a little more than a week now and still have a long voyage ahead I'm afraid. I got three letters from you today. They were dated July 16, 20, 22. You don't seem to have been receiving much mail from me. I didn't write much but it was more than you received or seem to have.

At any rate, I'm alive and well and kicking. Don't know where our destination is but I don't suppose I'll be seeing you for quite awhile.

I'm glad to hear the store is doing so well. Hope it gets better.

Don't know how much of this the censor will let get by but I suppose any is better than none. Love, Glade

Sgt. Glade M. Lyon—Co. B 3186 S.S.B.—APO 655 % PM NY NY

Written Aug. 2, 1945

Postmarked Sept. 5, 1945
Panama Canal Zone
Dear Folks.

I'm writing this from the Panama Canal Zone—and from the Pacific side of the isthmus at that—surprised? Me too. I didn't think they'd let us off the boat.

It's really nice here. Nice barracks with the first sheets I've seen in a long time. And a nice big P.X. with ice cream, coke, pineapples, coconuts, American girls and lots of other things I haven't seen for a long time.

They have some nice gifts here so I'll try and pick out something I think you may like and ship it.

I'm O.K. so don't worry. I'll write as soon as I get another chance. I wired you tonite. I imagine it will go right out. Love. Glade

Sgt. Glade M. Lyon—Co. B 3186 S.S.B.—APO 655 % PM NY NY

Aug. 30, 1945

Western Union
Jack Lyon.
Arrived Manila OK Tell Margee.
Glade Lyon

Sept. 5, 1945

Manila
Dear Folks

So here I am in Manila. I guess you got my radiogram. We

Sept. 5, 1945 *187*

arrived here the 28th of August and then I was on guard at the docks for several days.

We left Marseilles the 22nd of July and arrived at Panama the 2nd (I think). I sent you a cablegram from Panama. Also a bunch of gifts that they had on sale there. I suppose you got my letters from there too by now. I was lucky enough to get myself a new watch in Panama. It's waterproof, shock proof and antimagnetic. All for $16.25 at the P.X. Altogether I spent $70.00 in Panama and we were only there one night so you can see I had quite a spending spree.

When we got here I threw all my stuff on tshe truck when the first sserg. Told me I was on guard. And I've never seen my musette bag again. That doesn't matter much 'cause I can get more of the G.I. stuff but I had my binoculars in it and so I really hated to lose it. I guess Dad won't get the binoculars I promised him after all.

Prices here are very high. I don't know whether to try and buy you anything or not. Is there any certain kind of souvenier you'd like from the Phillipines?

We came over on the Monterey. It was a pretty good voyage although it took too long—36 days. It was quite crowded but the food was good.

I bought a monkey a couple of days ago. It's a very tiny female—only about three months old. We named it Murgatroyd. She's not housebroken but I still have hopes. I don't know whether I'll be allowed to take her back to the states or not but I'm going to try.

All my shaving equipment was in my musette bag so I'd appreciate it if you'd buy me a shaving brush and a Schick Injector razor. And be sure the razor is one that will open up. If you can gset me a box of 25 calibre automatic ammo I'd appreciate that too. I have a little 6.35 mm (25 cal) Mauser automatic pistol but no ammunition. I'd like a roll of cellophane tape too if you can do it.

I don't know where we go from here but I imagine it'll be Japan.

I'd sure like to come home tho. It seems like sort of a dirty deal that we have to stay here while the guys who went to the States from France don't have to come over here now. But there's not much we can do about it. Possibly if enough people yelled hard enough Congress might do something but I'm afraid that's the only way. I've only got 46 points.

Had an uneventful birthday. Don't seem any older at all hardly. Nuff said. Write soon. Love, Glade

Sgt. Glade M. Lyon—Co. B 3186 S.S.B.—APO 75 % PM San Francisco

Sept. 13, 1945

Manila

Dear Folks,

I haven't been writing nearly as often as I know I should. But it just seems that there is nothing to write. No news. Every day is the same. Get up about nine in the morning, play bridge or checkers or chess all day. In the evening we go to the Red Cross for a coke and if it's Mon., Wed. or Fri. we go to the movie. Go into Manila once in awhile but everything is so high we can't afford to buy much. For instance, a banana split costs $1.25. Sort of high, huh? It rains almost every evening but we're getting used to that.

Get Kay Hammond's address for me. I saw his name in the Red Cross register here. I might be able to look him up.

I've seen two of the boys I was in A.S.T.P. with. Stan Kordys was here yesterday and Don Grassi today. Love, Glade

Sgt. G. M. Lyon—Co. B 3186 S.S.B.—APO 75 % PM San Francisco

September 29, 1945

Lingayen Gulf
Luzon P.I.
Dear Folks,
We've moved again, but this time I didn't mind. Manila was O.K. but we didn't have very good living quarters. Here we have tents with wooden floors. But best of all is the beach and the ocean. It's wonderful. I can walk out in the ocean for over a hundred yards without getting in past my neck. There are lots of palms here and a very hot sun. Only thing missing are the beautiful native girls. But we have a lot of fun. This must be much the same ass the beach at Waikiki.

I got Connie's picture. She;s really grown up into a good looking gal. How old is she anyway? The fellows were wondering and I'm not sure. (Thanks a lot for the picture).

I sold Murgatroyd so I guess you won't get to see her after all. She was a lot of trouble and I was also afraid I wouldn't be able to get feed for her in Japan. On top of all that, it's sort of hard to get them into the States.

I don't expect to be leading for the U.S.A. until about Maarch ;or April. So don't expect me too soon.

As for Xmas presents, I have no idea for gifts for you so let's forget it for another year. I'll try to pick up something for Connie. That's about all for now. I'll write again soon. Love, Glade

Sgt. G. M. Lyon—Co. B 3186 S.S.B.—APO 315 % PM SanFrancisco, Calif.

Oct. 7, 1945

Lingayen Gulf

Well, we're still sitting here on the beautiful beach on the beautiful palms looking out over beautiful Lingayen Bay.

I haven't been writing much lately 'cause there's not much to write about. We don't go swimming as much anymore. The novelty has worn off a little and the typhoons that we got in the edge of made the breakers a little too big.

They made a jeep driver out of me the other day so I've been wheeling it round a bit. Nice for a change. But today they took the jeep away from me and gave me a 2 ½ ton truck (6 by 6) to drive. I'm a little afraid of it 'cause I haven't had much experience with them. I guess I'll get by tho.

I got a letter from Jim Barber the other day. He was transferred to an outfit all set to come over here. Then the Japs gave up so they were going home. Then those orders were cancelled about five minutes before they were to leave So now they're going to Germany I guess.

I got the pictures of Connie but I think I told you in the last letter.

I've only got 46 points and 28 months service so I don't expect to be home until about March. Love, Glade

Sgt. Glade M. Lyon—Co. B 3186 S.S.B.—APO 315 % PM—San Fran, Calif.

Oct. 10, 1945

Lingayen Gulf
Dear Folks,
Guess it's about time I wrote you another letter.

Yesterday we took a truck and went on a sightseeing trip to Baguio. It's the summer capitol of the Philipines. Ist's pretty high up in the mountains. The road was a lost like the one up past

Warm River only maybe a little crookeder and a lot rougher. The scenery was quite pretty but the town wasn't much to brag about. It's small (about 1500 I guess) and looks fairly modern but it's been pretty badly beaten up.

I got a letter from Grandpa and Grandma and they said Mother was going back to Mayo's again. Is that so? And why don't you tell me? Is it pretty bad? And why don't they fix it up once and for all?

I asked Grandpa if he could get me a Schick razor. You tell them what kind I want if they can get one. But I don't suppose they can.

Guess that's about all for today. There's not really much news. I'm waiting patiently for a box of cookies, Mom. How about it? Oh I forgot. I guess you're pretty busy and I don't really need the cookies. Sorry I asked. Love, Glade

Sgt. Glade Lyon—Co. B—3186 S.S.B.—APO 315 % PM—San Francisco, Calif.

Oct. 15, 1945

Lingayen Gulf
Dear Folks,
Here we go again! I'm on an LST that is going to weigh anchor and head for Kobe, Japan in a few hours. We came on board in trucks yesterday.

I don't know how long we'll be there or what we'll do. I suppose we're just part of the show of militaristic America that's being put on for the Japs.

I hope everything is O,K, at home. Let me know how Mom is. And how is the store coming along?

I'm O.K. as usual but awfully tired of moving around from one country to another. Don't ever let anyone try to tell you that anyplace is better than the U.S. I've been getting around quite a bit and there's no place like America.

England's standard of living is low. Only the upper classes have modern plumbing and central heating and electricity and automobiles. On the continent (Germany, France, Belgium you're more likely (but not that much more) to find these modern conveniences but the moral standards are extremely low. The Filipinos have more conveniences (in the cities) and have a fairly high moral code but they could certainly be clean and neat if they would try. I guess I'm getting homesick. I'm certainly sick of foreigners. Love, Glade

I'm enclosing a picture I've been been meaning to send. It's me and my roommates in our room In Eng.

Sgt. Glade Lyon—Co. B 3186 S.S.B.—APO 315 % PM—San Francisco, Calif.

October 18, 1945

Aboard L.S.T. 690
Lingayen Gulf
Dear Folks,

Got a letter from you and the Idaho Letter today. We were supposed to sail several days ago but for some reason or other we're still here. I hear we're leaving at seven in the morning tho.

So far it hasn't been bad being on board. We have pretty good food and cots to sleep on if we want them. I've been sleeping on the canvas top of my truck. We have movies every night and nothing to do all day. So we sleep all morning and play cards all afternoon. Usually we play bridge but this afternoon I made three dollars playing poker. Speaking of bridge, we think we're pretty good. There are four of us (Kuljiack, Borger, Korostoff and myself) who play together all the time. Day before yesterday four guys from another team challenged us and we beat them pretty badly. The next day I heard they were considered the champs in C Co. So you'd better get ready to play some bridge when I get home. As for playing poker—I know you don't like me to gamble but you should be resigned to the fact that I will anyway. I don't know whether you'll want to hear this or not, but I'll tell you just in case

November 4, 1945

you're afraid I'm losing (or gambling with) money I can't afford to lose. On the Monterey on the way over here from the ETO I got in a few crap games and ended up $180.00 ahead. Then about a week ago when we got paid there was another crap game and I made another $70.00. I hope you see I'm a bit ahead of course. I've spent a lot of it for things. Prices are very high all over and it doesn't take much buying to cut pretty deeply into $100.00. For instance, the stuff I bought in Panama cost me about $75. I sent $100 home a few days ago and I've got $100 in my pocket know. At any rate, I've got a lot to lose before I'm behind at gambling.

I'm awfully sorry to hear Mom's lip is bad again. Hope they can cure it for good this time.

I just haven't any idea on what to get Connie or Margee for their birthdays or Xmas. Margee's birthday is November 15, by the way.

Guess that's all for now. I have to mail this by 9:00. The trip will take eight days so you can expect an interval between this letter and the next. Love, Glade

Sgt. Glade Lyon
Co. B 3186 S.S.B.—APO 315 % PM—SanFrancisco, Calif.

November 4, 1945

Kobe, Japan
Dear Folks,

I got mother's letter from Rochester. I'm glad to hear her lip is O.K. now. Or at least I suppose its' O.K. now after the treatment.

We haven't been doing much here. We didn't have any money for several days so couldn't do any shopping. Yesterday we got out Jap money but I was on KP and today is Sunday and the stores are closed so a bunch of us are planning on going into Kobe or Osaka tomorrow and see what we can find. Is there anything you folks would like me to send you in the way of Japanese goods such as kimonos etc?

I cut this short to go to the movies. Just got back.

One of the fellows got a letter from his mother the other day in which she said "Gen. MacArthur is such a fine man." I'm wondering if you have the same misconception. Very few of the men over here have anything but hate for him. Most of that comes from his actions in the Philipines. MacArthur is a large property owner there and during the taking of Manila, he didn't allow the use of artillery in some places. To save his holdings from anymore destruction I suppose. What other reasons could he have? Not allowing the use of artillery made the taking of some strong-points such as the walled city in Manila, very difficult and cost more lives than was necessary. Of course, I may be wrong but I got it from men who were there when Manila was taken and they were very bitter about MacArthur.

I still don't know anything more about when I'll be home. I'm in the 6th Army so you can watch and see how fast they're sending 6th Army troops home. And I've got 46 points. But I think I've told you that before.

What is Eugene's address now and what is he doing? What about Lloyd Bratt? He's home so often I can't seem to keep track of him. I don't know what to get Connie for her birthday or for Xmas. I was thinking maybe I should just send money but since she's making so much in the spuds now, I guess that wouldn't be so good. How old will she bek this birthday anyway? Twelve? And how tall is she and how much does she weigh?

Guess that's enough for now. Love, Glade

I've been meaning to send this money home. I've sent you some before and I've sent Margee quite a bit. Save it for me will you? Some of these are notes the Japs printed with the intention of using them in the invasion of Australia (1 pound), America (dollars) and the Philipines (pesos). And some of it I carried from Europe. And I'm putting in two 1 yen notes. That's what we're using now. One yen is worth 6 2/3 cents.—Glade

T. Sgt. Glade Lyon—Co. B 3186 S.S.B.—APO 315 % PM—San Francisco, Calif.

Nov. 16, 1945

Dear Folks,

Got your letter of Oct. 30 today. I haven't written to you for a few days. I've been running around like mad the past few days. We found a building with a lot of Jap radio equipment in it and another with a lot of bombsights and other optical equipment. So we got a truck and hauled a bunch of it back to our barracks. We estimate conservatively $3000 of stuff. I'm going to try to send home a completer radio-transmitter-receiver. And some other parts. Don't know whether I'll be able to or not. One of the other guys (who lives in Miami) wants to send his to Ashton to and have you store it until he gets back. Will that be O.K.? I'll let you know if we get it in the mail. Ever since we got the stuff we've been busy taking it apart ad finding out how it works. I've got a couple of radios and a bunch of other electrical equipment. Also a bombsight, a machine gun camera and some other sights and lenses. More fun than a barrel of monkeys.

I sent another $100 a couple of days ago. I sure hope it's all been getting home. You should get $50 every month disregarding the amounts I tell you I'm sending. Do you?

There's not much to say. Still no prospects of getting home much before the middle of March. Looks like they would get us home faster if they'd put forth a little more effort.

This should reach you a little before Connie's birthday so I'll wish her a happy birthday right now. Sure wish I could get her something nice for her birthday.

Tomorrow is Saturday and there's a general coming to inspect us so guess I'd better close and get ready for him. Love, Glade

P.S.—There's a lot of talk about converting G.I. aftser your discharged. What do you suggest?

(Note from Dad—Glade has over $600 in his savings acct. now besides enough bonds to make it around a thousand dollars or more. Jack)

Sgt. Glade Lyon—Co. B 3186 S.S.B.—APO 315 ℅ PM—San Francisco

Thanksgiving (Nov. 25, 1945)

Kobe, Japan
Dear Folks,
Well, we had our Turkey dinner today but the best part of all was that we got a lot of mail for the first time in several days. It doesn't seem that I have a lot to be thankful for but I guess I should be very thankful that I'm alive and in one piece and have enough to eat. But we all want to be home so badly that it seems that nothing else matters.

I'm sorry to hear Mother is having so much trouble with her lip. Hope it's alright soon.

Just forget the cookies I asked for. I realize it's a lot of bother and they probably wouldn't be any good by the time they got here. In one letter you asked if I had received any of the packages the folks sent. I didn't know any had been sent. I haven't received any packages since before we left France.

I thought I told you to give the bracelets to Gwen and Velda but perhaps I didn't. One of these days I'm going to send you some fans for them too.

There's a golf course a few miles from here and I've been out several times. It's sure a lot of fun to get out and knock it around a little. But now I hear they're going to start giving us a lot of drill and stuff like that so I'm afraid we won't get a chance to go golfing much more.

I don't know what I'll do when I get out. I intend to go back to school (with the Gov't. paying me to). But I don't know where or when. I guess Margee and I will get married but I'm not even sure of that. Or where or when.

Guess that's enough for now. Love, Glade

Sgt. Glade M. Lyon—Co. B—3186 S.S.B.—APO 315 % PM—San Francisco

Nov. 29, 1945

Kobe, Japan
Dear Folks,
Guess it's about time I wrote you another letter. You've been asking for more info about the countries I'm in and right now I'm all het up about a couple of things so I'll tell it to you. I'm afraid I won't be able to say exactly what I want to but I'll try. The Japs are starving—not starving to death perhaps—but they're hungry—very hungry. Hungry enough to steal food. After we eat we wash our messkits outside and before we wash them we dump the stuff we didn't eat into a barrel. After a few hundred guys have thrown their leavings together it makes quite a mess. A mess whose odor is quite as repulsive as its appearance. But it hasn't been repulsive enough to keep the Japs from digging in with their hands to try to find something to eat. Nor to keep them from fighting with each other to get at the slop first. But now we've been given orders to keep them out. And I can't see that that at all. I think the U.S. should feed them. But if that is impossible, the least that can be done is to let them have anything we have left over. The Germans were hungry too for a while but then food kitchens were set up and every person got his or her ration of bread and soup every day. Every place I've been but Eng. there has been a big black market in cigarettes. But this is the first place I've seen that there has been any black market with food. When hungry people jump at the chance to pay $1.00 for a Baby Ruth they must be hungry.

Last night I was on guard. My post was the theatre—my orders were to keep the Japs out. I had to turn away about 40 Japs. All of them were very polite and several could speak English fairly well. I wouldn't mind if enough soldiers went to fill the theatre but there was an average crowd and there were still seats for about 150 persons.

Perhaps I'm too soft hearted but I hate to see people deprived of things because some officer thinks he or the U.S.A. is so much superior to the Japs.

Enough of that. The weather is pretty cold here. It rains fairly often. I don't know whether we'll have snow later on or not. I hope not.

They've got a big new program for us now. Our time has to be accounted for from 8 to 4 every day except Sat. (8 to 12) and Sunday. We have drill and calisthenics from 8 to 9;30 and then classes M. W. F. I take Abnormal Psychology from 9:30 to 10:30 and Philosophy from 10:30 to 11:30. T. & T. I play golf in the morning. In the afternoons I take Music Appreciation and take care of my truck and we're getting up a class in bridge. The only reason for all this is to keep us busy.

Playing golf here is a lot of fun. I get a pretty big kick out of it. I'm thinking of buying a set of clubs. I can get a set for Y700 ($47.50) and I think I could sell them in a few months without much loss.

Mom, would you like a kimono? A guy tried to sell me one tonight. It was about the nicest one I've seen. Good silk and embroidered partly with gold and silver threads. The real stuff. I offered Y600 ($42) but he said Y700 ($47) and so I said "no." It's very nice and if you'd like it I'll get it for you.

Time for bed. Love, Glade

P.S.—I'm enclosing two snaps we printed the other day. More in a week or so. They're not so good We didn't have the right stuff.

Sgt. Glade Lyon—Co. B. 3186 S.S.B.—APO 315 % PM—San Francisco, Calif.

Dec. 8, 1945

Kobe, Japan
Dear Folks,

I'm on guard tonight, but guess I can dash off a note between shifts. Today is four years from Pearl Harbor and the brass is afraid the Japs will try some sort of attack or sabotage, so the guard has been doubled and the Japs are being kept much farther away from the building than usual.

I got a package from Boyd and one from Velda yesterday. They are the first packages I've received for a long time.

Did I tell you about our school? I think so but I'm not sure. We go four hours a day (sometimes five) five days a week. I'm taking Abnormal Psychology, Philosophy, Bridge and Photography. I was taking Music Appreciation, but I dropped it in favor of photography. By the way, I'm getting to be quite a camera bug. So much so that some of the guys come to me for advice. I'm sending a picture that was taken with my camera while we enroute to Marseilles. I developed the roll quite a while ago and this afternoon I made and developed this enlargement. Pretty good picture huh?

I bought myself an enlarger a couple of days ago. I'll send it home as soon as I get it packed.

I'm trying to decide what to do with my camera. It's worth about $90 new in the states but I think I can sell it for $150 easily (maybe more). The camera I want costs about $225. I think I'll sell mine before I leave here and then buy the other one when I get home. Sounds like a lot of money huh? But I think you'll understand when I get home (I hope).

I got a few Xmas cards and sent them off yesterday. I could only get a few tho, so tell everybody hello for me.

I've got to get ready to go on guard again so I'll sign off. Love Glade

Sgt. Glade Lyon—Co. B 3186 S.S.B.—APO 315 % PM—San Francisco

Dec. 21, 1945

Kobe, Japan
Dear Folks,
I received your package a few days ago. Thanks a lot. I also got one from Velda, Boyd, and Margee. I'm saving them all up for Xmas. Ist isn't very far away either is it? In fact, it'll all be over when you get his. Tell me all about what you did.

I haven't written for quite awhile. Seems like there are never enough hours in a day for me to do everything. I've been on guard and K.P. since I wrote you and I have to drive my truck quite often and I have to take care of it. During the day we still have some classes. And at night we have movies or we go into Kobe and dance. And the time I have left over I spend in the darkroom developing and printing pictures of myself that I had a guy take a few days ago. It's not very good on account of we didn't have the right kind of printing paper. I'll try to send some other ones soon.

I've been sticking pretty much to one girl when I go down to Kobe to the dance hall. Her name is Sumiko. She's quite pretty and very sweet and I feel awfully sorry for her. Her parent's home was destroyed and she's working to pay off her father's debt. She's getting a little too attached to me tho. She wanted me to marry her but I told her I was going home soon. She cried for about an hour when she found that out.

Speaking of coming home—they're shipping the fellows out a little faster than I expected. At the rate they're going I should be leaving about January 15. So I should be home about six weeks from now. By the middle of February ar the latest.

Nuff for now. Love, Glade
Sgt. Glade M. Lyon—Co. B 3186 Sig. Sv. Bn.—APO 315 % PM—San Francisco, Calif.

Feb 12, 1946

Tacoma, Wash.
Dear Folks,
There are a few guys ahead of me at Ft. Lewis so they gave me a two day pass. I'm to get my discharge the 14th, but there can always be a hold-up so I'm keeping my finger crossed.

As I told you over the phone, I'm going to Moscow first, and talk the school situation over with the Dean and see what the living conditions are. Then home.

My tentative plans call for about two or maybe three weeks at home and then a journey to New York, stopping in Chicago to by a car and pick up a buddy and stopping in Bethlehem to pick up Margee. How does it sound to you?

The way things look right now, you can expect me about the 18th. That's not so long is it? Love, Glade

T/3 Glade M. Lyon—Co. C WDPC—Ft. Lewis, Wn.

GRANDPA GLADE'S RULES

To keep Grandpa Glade from being cantankerous, follow these Golden Rules for Living:

1. If you open it, close it.
2. If you turn it on, turn it off.
3. If you unlock it, lock it back up.
4. If you break it or lose it, admit it.
5. If you can't fix it, find someone who can.
6. If you borrow it, return it.
7. If you value it, take care of it.
8. If you make a mess, clean it up.
9. If you move it, put it back.
10. If it belongs to someone else, ask permission before you use it.
11. If you don't know how to operate it, leave it alone.
12. If it's none of your business, don't ask questions.
13. Throw garbage in the garbage can, not on the street.
14. Honor your mother and father.
15. Don't do dumb things.
16. Don't be late.
17. Do what you say you'll do, and when you say you'll do it.
18. Be happy.
19. Be nice.
20. Say "hello"; say "thanks"; say "you're welcome."

Glade's office

    21. Don't drive too fast. Watch out for the other idiot.
    22. Don't do anything that will hurt someone else's feelings.
    23. Don't steal.
    24. Don't lie.
    25. Love your family. Someday you'll find out that they are the most important part of your life.
    26. Don't cheat.
    27. Be honest.
    28. Trust everyone, but cut the cards.
    29. Realize that "There ain't no free lunch."
    30. Realize that "Them that has, gets."
    31. If it sounds too good to be true, it probably is.
    32. Don't do anything to anyone that you wouldn't want them to do to you.

33. Live the golden rule: Do unto others as you would have them do unto you.

34. Don't forget the other golden rule: The ones with the gold make the rules.

35. John Taylor Lyon said "Help the guy on the bottom of the pile—the one on top can take care of himself."

36. Don't do anything that you would be ashamed to tell your grandmother about.

37. Everyone should help make the world a better place to live.

38. Don't forget to vote.

39. Don't waste your money. A penny saved is a penny earned.

40. Grandma Miner said "Anything worth doing is worth doing well."

41. Always do your best at whatever you're doing.

42. If something needs to be done, do it now.

43. Sometimes you must leap; you can't cross a chasm in two small steps.
44. Enjoy life now—it's really a lot shorter than you think.
45. It never hurts to ask, the worst they can say is "NO."
46. Never strike a child except in anger.
47. If doesn't hurt anything, let them do it.
48. If it feels wrong, it probably is.
49. Don't apologize to your guests for anything.
50. Pay your debts.
51. Pay your own way.
52. Never quit learning on purpose.
53. Contain your anger, but spread your joy.
54. When you need something, buy the best you can afford.
55. Ask your children specific questions about their day.
56. The best therapy is _____ (huckleberrying, quilting, golfing, or ???). Do it whenever you can.

57. Keeping old friends is harder than making new ones.
58. Love life.
59. Love one another.
60. If someone offers you a breath mint, take it, they may know something you don't.
61. Put the toilet seat back down.
62. Don't drive too fast. Driving 25 miles at 10 miles an hour over the speed limit will save only five minutes.
63. Give an honest compliment whenever you can.
64. Always give your loved ones a gift at Christmas and on their birthdays even if it is only a verbal gift.
65. Appreciate what others do for you and let them know it.
66. Have a firm handshake.
67. Always hold the door open for your elders. Or anyone else, it won't hurt you a bit and it only takes a second.
68. Glade Lyon said "everyone should do his share of work to improve the community, but some must do more than their share because so many do so much less than their share.
69. Always ask the price. It may be a bargain.
70. To close a cardboard box, fold down the long side nearest you and then fold down the left side, and then the opposite side, and finally, fold down and tuck the last (right) side under the edge of the first side.

www.ingramcontent.com/pod-product-compliance
Lightning Source LLC
Chambersburg PA
CBHW071527040426
42452CB00008B/918